The Bitcoin Blitz © Copyright 2021 C. K. Spencer

All rights reserved

This book or parts thereof may not be reproduced in any form, stored in any retrieval system, or transmitted in any form by any means—electronic, mechanical, photocopy, recording, or otherwise.

Paperback ISBN-13: 979-8546616397
Hardcover ISBN-13: 979-8864348659
Audiobook ASIN: B09M969KBC
Ebook ASIN: B09BJYTH3S

Printed in the United States of America

© C. K. Spencer

Dedicated to my Mother, Father, and Spouse

The Bitcoin Blitz

The Past, The Present, and Future of Bitcoin

C. K. Spencer

Table of Contents

CHAPTER 1
The History Of This Relatively New Technology 1

How Did the Concept of "Cryptocurrency" Originate? 1

The History of Bitcoin 4

Technology.. 6

CHAPTER 2
How Blockchain Works 10

What is Blockchain and Distributed Ledger? 10

How Does Blockchain Technology Work? 13

CHAPTER 3
Types of Cryptocurrencies 18

Bitcoin 18

Ethereum 18

Litecoin 19

Ripple 19

Iota 19

Name... 20

Stellar Lumens 20

Cardano... 20

EoS (Ethereum-on-Steroids) 21

Tron... 21

Dash 21

Neo 22

Monero 22

Golem 22

Tezos 22

OmiseGo 23

DNotes 23

Zcash 23

Navin 24

Dogecoin 24

Stellar 25

CHAPTER 4
Cryptocurrency Wallet 26

Types of Cryptocurrency Wallets 29

CHAPTER 5
Cryptocurrency Keys 33

Public Key Cryptography (PKC) 33

Public Keys 34

Private Keys 35

CHAPTER 6
Cryptocurrency Exchanges 37

Types of Exchanges 37

LocalBitcoin 39

The Escrows 41

Exchange Platforms 42

Nuggets to Note While Choosing a Cryptocurrency Exchange
.... 45

CHAPTER 7
What You MUST Know Before Getting Started 49

Invest What You Can Afford to Lose 49

Do Not Get a Loan 50

Do Your Research 50

Set Realistic Expectations 50

CHAPTER 8
Cryptocurrency Mining 56

What is Mining? 56

There are Two Types of Cryptocurrency Mining Software: .. 62

Cryptocurrency Mining Pools: 63

The Process of Mining 64

The Secrets to Mining Cryptocurrency 64

Cryptocurrency mining is a principal activity. 65

The Perfect Coins to Mine 66

Alternative coins are increasingly picking up popularity 67

The Advantages of Bitcoin Mining 68

You get Free Bitcoin as a Reward 68

How Can You Make Money Offline with Cryptocurrency
Mining? 70

What Secrets Do You Wish to Learn About Cryptocurrency Mining?...71

CHAPTER 9
Different Investment Strategies 73

    Arbitration 76

    Hodl 78

    Trade 80

    Investing for the Long Term 83

    Investing for the Short Term 86

    Leveraging 89

    The Best Investment Strategy Includes:..................................94

    How Can You Profit from Investing in Cryptocurrencies? 99

CHAPTER 10
How To Choose A Crypto That Will Appreciate In Value........102

    Different Parameters to Consider When Choosing a Cryptocurrency to Invest in..102

    The Criterion to Choose a Cryptocurrency that will Appreciate in Value..105

CHAPTER 11
The Differences Between Bitcoin and Ethereum...................111

    Why Can Ethereum Grow Faster Than Bitcoin?....................113

    Why Will Bitcoin Always Remain the Most Prominent Cryptocurrency?...116

CHAPTER 12
What Is The Future Of Cryptocurrencies? 120

The Future of Decentralized Applications 125

CHAPTER 13
Cryptocurrency Scams 128

    Scams in Cryptocurrency Trading 128

    Investing Money Wisely 133

    How to Avoid a Scam in the Cryptocurrency Business 134

Conclusion 137

Preface

What is the first thing that comes to mind when you hear the terms "Cryptocurrency" or "Bitcoin?" If you are like most people I have talked to, you probably think "complicated" when you hear these terms.

Or maybe most of your friends are invested in cryptocurrency, and you are feeling behind and scared. Here, we will delve deeper into cryptocurrency basics, which will answer the most frequently asked question – "Should I buy cryptocurrency? – and how?"

When it first emerged in 2009, most financial and tech industries were at the forefront. For a long time, people did not seem to care much about it until its value grew to $19,783 in 2017! Everyone wanted to join in the trend. Since then, several other cryptos have emerged in the digital space, enhancing the competition.

Here, we will delve deeper into

- What cryptocurrency is and how it works
- An overview of its inner workings
- The different types of cryptocurrency
- The history of this relatively new technology

- How Blockchain works
- Different investment strategies
- Long-term vs. short-term
- The future of the crypto industry
- And so much more!

This book seeks to give you all the background information you need on this subject to have a solid understanding that will help you join the crypto family and start trading like a pro. Come with me, and let's get started!

Introduction

Over the past several years, cryptocurrencies have gained popularity. By 2018, there were more than 1,600 cryptocurrencies to trade – and the number is constantly growing. Cryptocurrencies have paved the way for an increase in demand for blockchain developers, and their salaries will tell you just how much they are valued. Research shows that full-stack blockchain developers earn more than $112,000 every month.

Are you interested in developing your career as a blockchain developer? Or perhaps you just want to learn how to trade cryptocurrency and grow your worth? This book aims at helping you reach your fullest potential.

In the past, people used the barter system to trade – exchange of goods and services between two or more people. For example, if you wanted apples and had strawberries, you would find someone who has what you want and wants what you have. Over the years, this barter system fell out of use because of its flaws:

1. People's requirements must coincide for a trade to happen. In other words, someone else has to want what you have and have what you want.

2. There is no standard measure of value, hence the need to decide how much you are willing to trade for what you want.

3. There is a challenge in the transportation of goods compared to the modern currency that perfectly fits your wallet or bank account.

Gold-plated florins replaced an official currency developed in 110 B.C. and became widespread in Europe and spread around the Globe. Perhaps you are wondering, "What is modern currency?" Modern currency includes coins, digital wallets, paper currency, and credit cards. Banks and governments control all these.

There is a centralized regulatory authority that limits how they work.

This brings us to the difference between traditional currency and cryptocurrency. Take a minute to think about it – suppose you want to repay a friend who helped you in a crisis by sending them money into their online account. That could go wrong in several ways:

1. You may suffer identity theft or denial-of-service-attack by hackers

2. The financial institution you are using to send money might have technical issues

3. There is a transfer limit you must not exceed when transferring money to another person's account

In short, there is a central point of failure, which is the bank! The good news is you have cryptocurrency, which is the future of currency. Supposing you have a similar transaction as above but now using the bitcoin app. You want to repay your friend using bitcoin, and all you have to do is confirm how much you wish to send to your friend. Once you get a notification and verify it, processing takes place – the system authenticates your ID, checks your balance in light of the transaction, and completes the process. All this takes place in a matter of minutes!

Do you see how cryptocurrency trumps all other means of payments? It eliminates all the problems faced by modern banking by offering no central point of failure and no limits on funds transfer.

So, what is cryptocurrency?

You can define cryptocurrency as a digital or virtual currency that serves as a medium of exchange. While it is pretty similar to real-world currency, cryptocurrency uses cryptography to work and does not have any physical embodiment. Because it works independently and in a decentralized manner – free from banks and central authorities – you can add new units once you meet the required conditions.

For instance, if you are mining bitcoins, you can only be rewarded a bitcoin once you add a block to the blockchain. It is the only way you can generate new bitcoins. The limit in the case of bitcoins is 21 million. Once this limit is reached, you can produce no more bitcoins. The good thing with cryptocurrency trading is that the transaction cost is low, considering there are no transfer fees charged when moving money from a digital wallet to a bank account.

Additionally, you can transact any time with no limits in your purchases and withdrawals. Cryptocurrency is free to use – not to mention the fact that international transfers are fast.

You are wondering, "what is cryptography?" It's a method of using decryption and encryption to secure communications, especially in the presence of third parties with ill motives, meaning no one can eavesdrop on your conversations, thanks to the computational algorithms used. A public key is used as a digital identity of the user, shared with everyone, and a private key that serves as a digital signature hidden from everyone else but the user.

In a typical transaction, the first thing that is key in the transaction details – whom you send the money to and how much you wish to send. The information is passed through a hashing algorithm – like SHA-256. After which, the output is passed through a private key to identify the user uniquely. Once the output is digitally signed, it's distributed across the network for user verification. The user will then check the transaction's validity before adding it to the blockchain, where no one can change details.

Chapter 1

The History Of This Relatively New Technology

How Did the Concept of "Cryptocurrency" Originate?

Cryptocurrency originated from a digital currency called "Bitcoin" in 2008. Bitcoins were designed to be "mined" on a computer giving the coin its unique capability of being entirely decentralized and peer-to-peer with no central authority or middleman required to authenticate transactions. The idea behind bitcoin's creation was to create a peer-to-peer electronic cash system online with no central authority to control it. So, if you have a website called "bitcoinslim.com," you could send value over the Internet to another person named "Joe Smith" without the need for a third party like PayPal or Western Union, and without needing to give them any of your personal information.

Bitcoin was introduced in 2009 by someone anonymously known as Satoshi Nakamoto, who went on to produce more than 1 million bitcoins from 2009-2011, which were each worth roughly $0.003 at the time of initial release. Bitcoin was to be a currency with no central authority or government. These characteristics of bitcoin made it very interesting to computer scientists, physicists, mathematicians, and others who wanted to create their types of "energy" in the form of a cryptocurrency.

In 2010 there were less than 1 million bitcoins in circulation, the mining rate increased by more than 300%, with that number rising to 6 million bitcoins per year by 2011. All this time, the bitcoin price remained static at around $0.008 US dollars. Following this period is when the absolute value of bitcoin started to rise. In late 2011, it was $1 per bitcoin, which made its total market cap worth less than 100 million dollars.

1) Bitcoins started being accepted by popular online retailers like Dell, Expedia, and eBay. Yet, these early adopters failed to see the potential in bitcoins. The price continued to rise as interest from new investors entered the market. In 2012, bitcoins reached a total market cap of 1 billion dollars, with its price at $13 per coin.

2) 2011-2013: A slow start with growing interest

The bitcoin price continued to rise steadily from 2012-2013 until it reached a record high of $1,200 in November 2013.

3) The rising cost of bitcoins attracted many people who wanted to buy bitcoins for investment purposes. The total number of bitcoins in circulation was still at 6 million at this point, meaning that each bitcoin was worth USD 0.20 and $3.98 billion.

4) Bitcoin's price increased by a factor of ten every year during this period, and its market cap grew by a factor of 100 each year. As interest grew, so did the centralization as new venture capital firms began to enter the market and take over mining facilities.

5) These venture capital firms raised their funds, recruited investors, hired developers, and competed with one another for BTC dominance. This was a problem because venture capital firms are centralized as opposed to decentralized. Whoever controls the most hashing power has the right to mine the most bitcoins. Venture capital firms raised hundreds of millions of dollars in funding so they could build extensive mining facilities and hire developers to create their mining hardware called ASICs.

6) These ASICs run at incredible speeds compared to CPUs or GPUs, which average home miners use.

7) Today, more than half of all hashing power and processing power is controlled by significant players.

Since these venture capital firms control so much hashing power and processing power, this gives them the right to mine most bitcoins per day. This centralization of mining is not the case in bitcoin's original design. Bitcoin's goal was to create a decentralized electronic cash system that was peer-to-peer with no mining centralization or companies controlling more than 50% of the hashing power.

8) In 2013, some members of the community felt that these centralized companies were corrupting bitcoin, so they tried to work on alternative cryptocurrency projects with the hopes of improving upon bitcoin. Bitcoins had already become extremely popular, so it wasn't hard for other cryptocurrency projects to find followers and pick up where Bitcoin left off. The first group to do this in a big way was called "Bitcoin Cash," which took place in 2015.

9) Bitcoin Cash was a hard fork of bitcoin, which launched with 8MB block sizes (as opposed to Bitcoin's 1MB). It gave Bitcoin Cash an advantage over Bitcoin in the mining process as it had larger blocks.

The History of Bitcoin

Bitcoin originated from the 2008 global financial crisis due to banks and governments mismanaging the economy with their reckless use of money printing.

Cryptocurrencies are currencies that a single entity cannot control. They use cryptographic techniques to secure the transactions and control the creation of new units, and they are utterly transparent to their users. Therefore, they offer great promise for being used as alternative currencies in the future. Natural selection dictates that the currency best adapted to its environment would become the most prevalent in its niche; thus, cryptocurrencies are based on supply-and-demand economics.

This gives cryptocurrency markets a unique advantage over traditional markets. When demand increases, it will be met with an increase in supply, unlike gold historically where growing demand has reduced supply. In 2012, Bitcoin became the first decentralized cryptocurrency when Satoshi Nakamoto released it. In January 2014, a record number of bitcoins were created when the solution to a proof-of-work problem was found by an unknown person or group of people. In September 2015, however, the creation rate dropped to approximately 6.25 bitcoins per hour.

The bitcoin network is based on mathematical proof called "hashing" that enables bitcoin tumbler services to create new currency units or verify transactions without a trusted third party. This system has built-in redundancy and guarantees that the money will not be duplicated even if every computer in the bitcoin network fails simultaneously. The bitcoin network has proven that it can be well adapted even in adverse environments such as during the global financial crisis of 2008 or in countries that experience hyperinflation since its value has been resilient to market fluctuations.

Technology

Blockchain technology is the process of using a decentralized, distributed, and public digital ledger for recording transactions across many computers so that there is no alteration of record retroactively without altering subsequent blocks and the collaboration of the network.

The initial term "blockchain" described a structure that records all bitcoin transactions; blockchain is now used to record any transaction. This makes blockchain technology applicable to many industries. Some specific applications include healthcare management (via electronic medical records), banking, insurance claims processing (via smart contracts), and real estate. Given the ability of blockchain technology to create an immutable record of all transactions, it could play a key role in documenting historical events and solving other historical problems.

The network that serves these applications is known as the "blockchain" network.

Cryptography is a method for exchanging sensitive documents and information confidentially. The critical feature of cryptography is its reliance on math instead of trust. Mathematics provides a way to encrypt and decrypt data while still verifying the integrity of the data with digital signatures or some other kind of digital signature. Cryptography relies on three elements:

1) A mathematical algorithm
2) An encryption key

3) The receiver's public encryption key for verification purposes

Cryptography uses public-key encryption to ensure confidentiality.

Digital signature algorithms are used to validate the integrity of data. One algorithm that is commonly used is a widely known algorithm called RSA.

Public key cryptography is a subset of symmetric and asymmetric cryptography that uses a public key and a private key. The public key can be freely distributed and will never be known by anyone other than the owner. In contrast, the private key must be kept secret at all times. Public keys help ensure authenticity by allowing one entity to communicate with another entity while keeping their identity secret.

The messages are then encrypted with the private key and decrypted with the public key. The private key should only be used to decrypt messages encrypted with the entity's public key. While this ensures the confidentiality of communication, it does not necessarily protect data integrity; someone can intercept the message and then modify it without anyone else knowing.

Cryptography is a form of secure communication in which information such as passwords are converted into unreadable digital data. Cryptography provides identification, privacy, and authentication on an agreed-upon system so that users can prove their identity by ensuring each message they send appears as they intended.

To keep data secure, encryption techniques convert the data into a stream of unreadable characters known as ciphertext. Without an encryption key, anyone intercepting the message cannot decipher it. The sender uses an encryption algorithm and their private keys to encrypt the information making up the message.

To decrypt the information, one needs a decryption key and an encryption system that matches the sender's message. Asymmetric cryptography is a form of cryptography based on two keys: a public key and a private key. The public key is available to everyone and can be used for encrypting messages but for decryption, one must have access to its paired private key, which must be kept secret. Often the public key is distributed widely to everyone in the network and kept on a public key infrastructure (PKI) server. The private key must be kept secret and secure by its owner. Otherwise, anyone can use it to decrypt messages sent to that owner; otherwise, the system is useless.

A digital signature algorithm is used for validating data integrity. One widely used algorithm is called RSA. The private key ensures that no one else will be able to read your data, while the public key serves as an address that everyone can read but only written to only by you. The sender generates a unique hash. This hash is created by taking their private key and running a mathematical process on the key to producing a digital signature. The sender then sends this digital signature to the recipient. To check the signature's authenticity, the recipient must compare the cryptographic hash of the message sent with that of his or her secret key provided to him or her in advance. If they match, he or she knows that there was no modification of any kind in that data (therefore, no embezzlement).

If one's private key is stolen, every message encrypted with it will have its public key used instead of their private one, effectively embezzling from themselves. If a hacker breaks into a computer system and steals private keys, he or she has easy access to all data sent to the owner of that key. Though this cannot happen in an internet-connected system using asymmetric cryptography, it is common in private networks with weak security controls.

Digital signatures provide authentication of data integrity and authenticity; other technologies such as hashing can accomplish these goals. Hashing algorithms take user-supplied data (the message) as input and generate a unique identifier known as a hash (a one-way function). A hash is generated for every binary block of computer memory (e.g., for every bit), whether or not the contents change. The advantage of hashes is that they are completely reversible. If a hash is known to be correct, the original message can be recovered by running the same algorithm on the data with which it was initially hashed.

The problem with hashes is that they may take a long time (gigabytes or even terabytes) to calculate, and even then, one must know in advance what algorithm will be used. This makes hashes useful for intentional tampering: once a hash value is calculated for a given message, the original data never needs to be recovered.

Chapter 2

How Blockchain Works

What is Blockchain and Distributed Ledger?

Bitcoin, and most cryptocurrencies that came after it, employ a brand-new technology called Blockchain. In simple terms, it is just an accounting ledger of all transactions ever to have been completed by every person ever to have used bitcoin. Think of it as a giant filing cabinet. Each file in each drawer contains transaction details for a certain period, which in the case of bitcoin is roughly every ten minutes and 500 transactions worth. The files, one after another, are placed sequentially in a drawer and kept forever. Think of each file as a 'block' and link these blocks sequentially together in a physical chain - or blockchain. Thus, the entire filing cabinet is the blockchain. The same technique can be used for any number of applications that require a secure record of any transaction or data. It's the ultimate secure and decentralized solution to many problems.

Cryptographic techniques are used to verify and link these transactions using a 'Hash Function.' Data from the previous block is computationally hashed together (or mixed) with the new block, using cryptographic methods. These are hashed with the block before that, so that it cannot be undone. The algorithms contain an impossible-to-unravel computation of long alphanumeric sequences combined with public and private 'keys.' The technique is called public and private key cryptography. A bitcoin owner holds an electronic or printed paper 'wallet' with a public key and a private key. The latter proves ownership, like a password, since the bitcoin owner keeps it secret, and it cannot be unraveled from the other data in the hash. The public key can be handed out for others to pay into, similar to you giving me your bank account number. As long as the private key is kept secret, the cryptocurrency is safe and only ever accessible by that one person. A private key is a random 256-bit number, equating to 64 hexadecimal characters in a row when written down. So it would take approximately 0.65 billion years to crack with existing computing technology. In terms of the number of 'tries,' that's one followed by 77 zeros (2^{256})! Let's write that in full for maximum effect

100,000,000,000,000,000,000,000,000,000,000,000,000,000,000,000,000,000,000,000,000,000,000,000,000,000.

So it's safe then, just as long as you keep that private key safe! We'll get to how to secure this safely later in the book. But here comes the clever bit that we alluded to in the last chapter. Identical copies of the entire ledger are contained in thousands of different computers worldwide so that there is no single point where the data is stored. Hence no single attack vector. Any change in the Blockchain needs to be verified by other nodes on the network and be present on all copies worldwide. This makes it impossible to hack or change, as you cannot hack all of them at once. You might be able to change one or two versions of the data, but you won't be able to change them all – almost 100,000 nodes now, in the case of bitcoin.

This is called a distributed ledger, and it runs on a decentralized network. Decentralization is the buzzword, the key to everything, and it underpins bitcoin's technology and most of the blockchain movement. It is that which gives it trustless and uncompromised properties. Banks have their way of storing databases of transactions. However, this is usually highly centralized, in a specific building or on one particular single set of servers, entirely controlled by only a few people. This makes it prone to hacking, with a much lower attack vector of, at most, a few machines. It also gives a single institution complete control of your assets and costs, not to mention forcing you to use dinosaur money.

Bitcoin, by comparison, is controlled by tens of thousands of people. It is worth noting here that not all cryptocurrencies are decentralized like this. A lot is owned and managed by a corporation or single entity. With its anonymous and open source (free to all) code, it is different.

As such, it cannot be stopped by any government, law or organization, unless the entire Internet was shut down. It is out there and out there to stay. Plus, the biggest blockchain is generally the safest because of the enormous amount of data you need to unravel to pick it apart.

How Does Blockchain Technology Work?

Blockchain is a technology that can make power transactions for everything from currency to documents of ownership. Think of it as a decentralized ledger that stores a list of transactions that cannot be erased or tampered with and is fundamentally secured by cryptography.

How Does Blockchain Work?

1. The transactions are stored in what's referred to as "blocks." A block is a collection of data chained together using cryptographic hash functions to ensure security. Since each block in the chain requires high security, it can only be added or removed once verified by other miners (permitted participants), and those blocks require proof of work.

2. Once a transaction is added to the Blockchain, it's verified by a network of participants (miners). These miners use the most powerful computers on the market today, referred to as "nodes," to verify transactions. This is what gives Miners an incentive to add more transactions to the chain and keep it secure.

3. Since each block contains cryptographic hash functions, it's impossible for one person or entity to change a particular block without others noticing. However, if someone tries, they're easily detected because of the way that blockchain works - all nodes in the network will record a new block when they see one that is different from their own (this process is called "mining").

4. The blockchain ledger can be shared among a distributed network of computers. This is the key to its security because even if a hacker could get in and access the ledger, they would have no way to change it without alerting everyone else on the network. Additionally, anyone with access to the blockchain network should be able to see what's stored in it.

5. There are thousands of computers worldwide that form people's nodes on the network, which are connected 24 hours a day. These computers are called "miners." Miners' job is to run software which verifies transactions and adds them onto the Blockchain. Miners are rewarded for their work with cryptocurrency (bitcoin).

6. The blockchain is not any one thing. It's an idea that anyone can use to create a digital ledger. For example, an open-source project uses the blockchain concept to record transactions in the diamond industry. This technology has enormous potential for other applications, like tracking medical records or securing land title records worldwide.

7. blockchain technology upholds decentralized control as opposed to centralized electronic money and central banking systems.

8. Blockchain is a decentralized ledger. It is a technology that facilitates the safe transfer of money, information, and assets on a public network that can be viewed and audited by anyone.

9. A blockchain takes the trust out of transactions and maintains it in the network so that no one party can change information without others noticing.

10. The blockchain ledger can be shared among a distributed network of computers worldwide without any central authority controlling it (hence its security).

11. A blockchain stores a decentralized list of database entries shared among several computers for verification. Thus, a single set of transactions cannot be altered without everyone else seeing it.

12. Blockchain technology upholds decentralized control as opposed to centralized electronic money and central banking systems.

13. In addition to that, anyone with access to the blockchain network should be able to see what's stored in it, allowing them to verify that the information is accurate and true.

14. The Blockchain concept is open-source, meaning other individuals or groups could use this same technology and build upon it with various ideas, creating a wealth of possibilities for this technology as an enabler for

different applications beyond payments and records like land ownership.

Blockchain technology can be used to record any kind of transaction or agreement. Examples include:

1. Document history - Using a blockchain, you can track all the changes made to a file like a PDF or a photo, and any time there is a change, everyone else in the Blockchain will see it.

2. Record land transactions - Ubiquity plans to use blockchain technology in Brazil to track real estate transactions.

3. Legal application - Law firms are currently exploring how to leverage Blockchain's ability to create permanent indisputable proof of legal agreements.

4. Online gambling - Betting Skull is testing the Blockchain for online gambling applications and is creating an online application that will allow gamblers to deposit funds using bitcoin or other cryptocurrencies.

5. Medical records - MedRec is working on a solution in which doctors can use blockchain technology to securely share information with patients about their medical conditions and their medications.

6. Land title record distribution - Real estate management firm Propy recently launched the world's first government-recognized title registration service on Blockchain. This makes it easier for sellers to access

their property records and title deeds without going through banks or other expensive third parties.

7. Charity - Charity organizations are exploring the Blockchain's ability to process donations and provide donors with the certainty that their donation is going where it's supposed to.

In summary, blockchain technology can be used to record any kind of transaction or agreement. For example, document history; record land transactions; legal applications; online gambling; medical records; land title record distribution; and charity.

Blockchain technology has many potentials to be used in the healthcare industry since it provides transparency and security for medical records and medical information. This technology has enormous potential for other applications, as mentioned above in section 3 (like tracking diamond transactions).

Chapter 3

Types of Cryptocurrencies

Before we delve deeper into cryptocurrency trading, we must discuss the different types of cryptocurrencies. Here, we will discuss the most commonly used cryptocurrencies, which include:

Bitcoin

Bitcoin is the first cryptocurrency created in 2009. Some of the reasons people love bitcoin are low transaction costs, anonymity, independence from institutions like governments and banks, and decentralization - meaning no single person or group can control it.

Ethereum

Ethereum is a cryptocurrency that offers additional features beyond those offered by bitcoin. There are plans to create a distributed autonomous corporation (i.e., a decentralized independent organization represented by computer encoded rules and governed by users, not a central authority) using Ethereum and exchanging contracts using blockchains. Many major corporations have expressed interest in using Ethereum's services; for example, Toyota has agreed to work with the Ethereum team on developing self-driving cars.

Litecoin

Litecoin is a fork of Bitcoin, created in 2011 by Charlie Lee (who would later found Coinbase). It is similar to Bitcoin but easier to use for smaller payments and fast confirmations. It also has a more rapid block generation speed, which means that transactions are confirmed more quickly.

Ripple

Ripple is a cryptocurrency and payment network that targets banks and global payments rather than individuals. In addition to sending currency between two parties instantly (similar to PayPal or Venmo), it includes some features that would appeal to banks: instant confirmations, additional anonymity, and the ability for currency exchange.

Iota

IOTA is an open-source cryptocurrency explicitly designed for machines in the "Internet of Things" environment. This growing technology area involves connecting devices like cars, appliances, and networks to improve their functionality. Some of the uses include electric car battery charging, smart appliances ("smart" fridges that can order groceries when supplies run low or connected washing machines that can alert you when a load is done), and self-driving cars.

Name

NEM is an ambitious cryptocurrency platform that hopes to offer many services beyond simply being a currency. Its goal is to be "the new shiny Bitcoin." It provides a wide variety of messaging, asset trading, encrypted messaging, voting systems, and more.

Stellar Lumens

Stellar Lumens is similar to Ripple but easier to use and free for institutions like banks and remittance companies. Stellar Lumens are currently used by IBM's blockchain services, Deloitte, and the National Bank of Abu Dhabi.

Cardano

Cardano is a cryptocurrency designed specifically for use in developing nations and not just for individuals. Smart contracts are an essential portion of the Cardano system, enabling automatic bill paying and smart government benefits distribution. Its founder, Charles Hoskinson, is also the co-founder of Ethereum.

EoS (Ethereum-on-Steroids)

EoS provides a solution to issues of scalability facing Ethereum and other cryptocurrencies in the market. It offers more transactions per second and doesn't require as much RAM as Ethereum to run. BlockOne, the team behind EOS, has already released several products; the most popular cloud storage provider is BitShares.

Tron

Tron is another ambitious cryptocurrency project aimed at the entertainment industry with decentralized storage and smart contracts for ticketing. It's led by famous Chinese entrepreneur Justin Sun, formerly involved in Ripple Labs (and created Peiwo, an audio-based social media app with ten million users).

Dash

Dash is a cryptocurrency that bids "immediate" transactions, "private" transactions, and an optional decentralized governance system. Dash developers believe that these features make it ideal for smaller purchases (like those made at the grocery store).

Neo

NEO was started by Da Hongfei, a famous Chinese entrepreneur who founded several companies, including OnChain, a startup focused on blockchain projects in China. NEO is similar to Ethereum but aims to do more for the Chinese government while staying out of China's regulatory jurisdiction.

Monero

Monero is a newer cryptocurrency that improves on some of the privacy issues surrounding Bitcoin. It uses something called ring signatures to make transactions anonymous.

Golem

Golem is another cryptocurrency project focused on "global marketplaces" for buying and selling CPU power used for computations and data analysis or, in some cases, for running apps that need a lot of computing power (like video rendering or machine learning). The goal is to create "the first decentralized supercomputer."

Tezos

Tezos' main goal is to create a new governance model for cryptocurrencies rather than rely on Bitcoin Beeker donations. It's helmed by Arthur and Kathleen Breitman (husband and wife). It was embroiled in a scandal over the tech it was founded upon. Because of that, we are yet to know whether it successfully solves the governance problem.

OmiseGo

OmiseGO focuses on creating "the new financial system" through cryptocurrencies. Which they hope will disrupt the existing financial system in underdeveloped countries like Thailand or Vietnam.

DNotes

DNotes is a digital currency that includes some extra features, including a rewards program and a wiki for newcomers to learn about cryptocurrencies.

Zcash

Zcash is similar to Monero but includes zk-SNARKs, making it a privacy-protecting digital currency. It transacts efficiently and safely, with low fees, while at the same time making sure digital transactions remain private. Unlike most cryptocurrencies that reveal your transaction history and holdings to the public, Zcash transactions are confidential.

While the transaction data is posted to a public blockchain, you have the option of confidential transactions and financial privacy through shielded addresses. The good thing with zero-knowledge proofs is that they allow transaction verification without necessarily exposing the sender, receiver, or amount you are transacting. This way, you share some transaction details for compliance or audits only.

Navin

Navin was established in 2014 - without pre-mine or ICO - and has stood the test of time. It has seen features added since its inception, improvements made, and upgrades to its codebase. This factor and its dedicated team ensure NavCoin continues to grow consistently.

NavCoin was built on the Bitcoin Core code, albeit with several changes. One such change was adding a sub-chain to the main blockchain, which is called NavTech, and it is what enables mixing and the anonymization of transactions on the NavCoin blockchain. Another change was to replace Bitcoin's proof of work algorithm with proof of stake. Compared with Bitcoin, NavCoin is a lot faster and cheaper.

Dogecoin

Dogecoin was formed as a meme and is now the 26th largest Cryptocurrency globally by market cap (it's worth about $623 million). Legendary "Shibe" Shibetoshi Nakamoto was part of the group that launched Dogecoin. It's a popular cryptocurrency, but it's not one for serious investors.

Stellar

Stellar is a cryptocurrency that seeks to connect all payment systems (like PayPal, ACH, or wire transfers) and lets them use an international currency called Lumens for transactions. It aims to be a complete transaction solution that can work with every existing payment method and currency worldwide.

Chapter 4

Cryptocurrency Wallet

"I am very excited about the prospect of using cryptocurrency, not just as a money equivalent, but using it as a way to earn something as a result of doing some type of work."

– William Mougayar

There are specific steps you must take to start your trading experience. The first step is to decide what cryptocurrency wallet will be the best for you. To do this, you must understand what a crypto wallet is, what it is used for, and what makes a crypto wallet standard and suitable for trading. Aside from this, you must then understand the concept of cryptocurrency exchanges and identify the best way for you to trade your crypto coins.

In this chapter, we will discuss the merits and pitfalls of various crypto wallet services.

Cryptocurrencies like Bitcoin (BTC), Ethereum (ETH), Tether (USDT), Litecoin (LTC), etc., cannot be stored without a crypto wallet. And if you can't store crypto without a wallet, you definitely cannot trade either. There are various types of crypto wallets where you can collect and keep your crypto coins. However, it is more important to choose the best of these different crypto wallets to suit your trading needs and preferences.

So, what is a crypto wallet? Crypto wallets are remarkably similar to how a vending machine works in a public place. Simply put, anyone can put cash into the vending machine. Yet, you can only take out money from the vending machine if you have the keys. This is how crypto wallets or digital wallets work.

Before you begin any trading or investment with any type of cryptocurrency, it is required that you get a space where you can store your crypto coins. That space, where you can lawfully confirm the presence of your cryptocurrencies and quickly find out your crypto balance, is what is referred to as crypto or a digital wallet.

Digital wallets or crypto wallets contain two kinds of keys (private keys and public keys). These keys are what run the primary activity that takes place in your crypto wallets. These special keys are used to receive cryptocurrencies and likewise send to other crypto wallets. They are similarly used to perform certain transactions on the blockchain system.

It is general knowledge that cryptocurrencies are not concrete items. Likewise, all trades performed through these cryptocurrencies make up the digital ledgers you find on the blockchain system. So, a type of password is required to verify the presence of cryptocurrencies on the blockchain system. This is where private, and public keys come into play.

Every crypto wallet account comes with a unique address. This address is the crypto equivalent of the IBAN used in physical banking processes. Therefore, if you want someone to send you money, you do not need to share any other details than your crypto wallet address.

Private and public keys are employed as passages to the deposits made into the crypto wallet account. They are again used to send money from the crypto wallet account to another account. It is impossible to perform any transaction without either the private and the public key. Blockchain technology requires at least one of these two keys before any transaction can take place. Specific unique encryption standards are used to link the public and private keys together. Due to this, you can access the public key information using the private key. But you cannot access the private key information using the public key.

In the cryptocurrency community, the private key is regarded as the most strong password. If this private key is gotten by anyone aside from the crypto wallet account holder, all cryptocurrency deposits may be forfeited. It is always impossible to get these deposits back. Thus, it would be best if you kept the private key safe and confidential. You must further ensure that no other person aside from you accesses this key.

A cryptocurrency wallet is a software program, a hardware gadget, or an online platform where the public and private keys are stored.

Types of Cryptocurrency Wallets

There are several kinds of cryptocurrency wallets. This segment will explain the various crypto wallet technologies available and the pros and cons of using them.

Hardware Wallets

These are one of the most secure ways to keep cryptocurrencies. They are also referred to as "cold wallets." They are used offline, making them a safer storage facility than "hot wallets" (which includes web wallets and software wallets).

Pros

- They deliver increased in-built protection as you cannot access them without the correct password.
- They have excellent storage facilities.

Cons

- It is an expensive type of cryptocurrency wallet. Yet, it tends to offer real value for your money.
- When they get corrupted, it might be impossible to retrieve all that is in them. The same happens if you forget your passcode. If you think it can't get any worse, there's the story of Stefan Thoman. He forgot

the password to his bitcoin wallets worth over $220 million.

- As physical storage devices, the chances are that you might misplace them.

Examples of recommended hardware Wallets you can use are:

- Ledger Nano S
- Trezor wallet
- KeepKey

Software Wallets

Software crypto wallets are also known as "hot wallets." This is because they are used through the internet. Unfortunately, this remote use makes them victims of hacks and cyber-attacks. However, if you plan to trade in low quantities, desktop software crypto wallets would be perfect for you!

My number one recommended software wallet would be Coinbase. This is due to the numerous perks it provides to you as a crypto trader. Other recommended software wallets include:

- Electrum (not for beginners due to its technicalities)
- Exodus

Mobile Phone Wallets or App-based Wallets

Mobile phone wallets or app-based wallets are the most popular types of crypto wallets. And from their name, they are used on phones as applications. Binance is a first-choice mobile phone wallet for most cryptocurrency investors. The reasons are undeniable. Binance hosts the largest cryptocurrency exchange in the world, as you must now know. It also runs its Smart Chain and meager transfer fees, unlike other blockchains. Others include Jaxx Liberty, Mycelium, Copay, and Cryptonator.

Web Wallets

Web wallets are not entirely safe. Here, the reality is that you never get access to your private keys. Therefore, we recommend them only as a temporary space to move cryptocurrencies from one place to another. Regardless, it still all boils down to how well you trust whichever provider you choose.

With hacking incidents that befell Mt. Gox and Coincheck in 2020, Coinbase is the only provider I can recommend in this category.

Paper Wallets

Paper wallets will easily pass as one of the most secure ways of keeping your Cryptocurrency safe. They are used offline to hold cryptocurrencies. It is precisely the printing of QR codes that stand for your private and public keys. This offline safety system implies that you have complete custody of your cryptocurrencies. Paper wallets are one of the best cryptocurrency wallet setups out there!

However, you should note that a paper wallet will not be the best option for every crypto trader. If you plan to trade every day or every week, paper wallets are not the best for you. This crypto wallet setup is most suitable for those who want to be long-term cryptocurrency investors. Additionally, you must exercise caution when using this wallet. Any damage, either through water, fire, or any other kind, can lead to you losing all your digital assets and investments.

In all, hot wallets (desktop software wallets and app/web-based wallets) are not wholly secure crypto wallet options. They are only suitable for small-scale trades. Cold wallets (hardware wallets and paper wallets), on the other hand, are safer options and will work well for long-term investors. Your responsibility is to decide the wallet that works best for your type of investment.

Chapter 5

Cryptocurrency Keys

As stated earlier in this book, keys are an essential cryptographic concept used to lock and unlock different cryptographic functions. There are several other cryptographic keys, but the keys in wallets necessary for sending and receiving cryptocurrencies are the public and private keys.

The private and public keys help to verify crypto transactions without the need for a third party. Private and public keys are significant concepts in the public key cryptography (PKC) framework.

Public Key Cryptography (PKC)

Public Key Cryptography (PKC) is also known as asymmetric cryptography, a specialized system in cryptography that uses long alphanumeric keys that work together in pairs — private and public keys. These pairs of alphanumeric keys are generated with cryptographic algorithms that run on one-way mathematical functions.

The mathematical model is known as trapdoor functions, which can only be solved in one particular way and almost impossible to crack any other way. Once these functions are built, reverse engineering them is only possible with a supercomputer that might have to run for several thousand years.

In simpler terms, PKC can be described to validate and authenticate anything using asymmetric encryption. PKC technology was initially used for encrypting and decrypting messages before they became relevant in cryptocurrency for encrypting and decrypting transactions.

Now cryptocurrency transactions are impossible without the public and private keys generated by the PKC. While the public key can be distributed to others, private keys should never be disclosed to anyone besides the owner. Public keys store cryptocurrencies, send or receive cryptocurrencies in conjunction with their corresponding private key.

Public Keys

A public key is one of the long alphanumeric pairs generated by the PKC, and as the name implies, it is the only part that can be shared with the public. The public key is a cryptographic code paired to a private key that allows users to send and receive cryptocurrency transactions. Though you only need the public key to initiate a transaction to and from a wallet, you need a private key to prove that you have ownership of the cryptocurrencies created by the transactions.

The term "wallet address" is sometimes used in the crypto space to describe the public key when a user needs to receive a transaction. However, the wallet address is a hashed version of the public key, shortened to make crypto transactions more convenient for users.

You can freely share your public key with the public to receive cryptocurrencies or blockchain assets. When public keys are released to the public, anyone can easily send crypto assets in them. For example, you might have seen charity homes and some organizations display their wallet addresses online for people to make donations to them.

Private Keys

A private key is the other pair of keys generated by the public key cryptography. Private keys are the entities that serve as proof of ownership for cryptocurrencies stored in crypto wallets. They also give you the ability to spend cryptocurrencies that belong to your public address.

Private keys are typically large numbers that can be paired with public keys in varying forms. These include:

- The 256-character extended binary code
- Mnemonic phrase (seed)
- The 64-digit hexadecimal code

- The quick response code (QR)

Irrespective of the form the private keys are assigned, you should never disclose them to anyone.

Due to the one-way mathematical algorithm used in generating cryptographic keys, it is practically impossible to generate a private key with a public key. However, it is possible to generate public keys with a private key, making it possible to have multiple public keys assigned to a single private key.

As the name implies, a private key must always remain private. Never share this with anyone because whoever has access to your private key can access all the cryptocurrencies associated with the keys. Therefore, keeping your private keys confidential, safe, and secure will forever remain one of the best safety measures you can take in the crypto space.

Chapter 6

Cryptocurrency Exchanges

This is where to buy, sell, and trade your cryptocurrencies. It is imperative to note that crypto exchanges are not built similarly. You must consider certain factors when deciding whether a cryptocurrency exchange can satisfy your unique set of needs as a crypto trader. These factors to be considered include:

- The type
- The features
- The security regulations in place

Types of Exchanges

Brokerage

Some exchanges permit traders to buy or sell straight from the platform. This gives room for one-time trades and is most suitable if you are just beginning to trade. Investors are usually required to verify their investment accounts by submitting personal identification details.

Peer-to-Peer

Commonly referred to as P2P, these platforms work perfectly for those primarily concerned with their privacy. In addition, peer-to-peer exchanges permit one-on-one trading relationships where two traders select a particular price and mode for payment independently.

Some P2P exchanges are classified according to location. That way, you get to meet other crypto traders at a particular geographical point. Most P2P platforms proceed slightly by fostering the trade and functioning as escrow and mediator when there is a disagreement. Your privacy is generally guaranteed on these platforms. Still, the burden of your security and that of your cryptocurrencies is on your shoulder.

Full Trading Platform

Full trading platforms create an environment featuring many traders coming together to trade among themselves on the platform, just as it is in an actual stock market. Full trading exchanges employ an order book to buy and sell orders correspondingly. The more prominent full trading platforms even deliver several features such as margin trading, particular order types, customizable graphs, etc. As a beginner trader, you will not need most of these features.

With the birth of Bitcoin, the need arose to exchange the new cryptocurrency with fiat currency.

Over time, some traders began to accept this new form of payment; they too needed to convert that profit made in BTC into legal tender currency. Even the most avid supporters, those who have kept their BTC longer, have also had the opportunity to spend them over time.

Spending cryptocurrencies is now extremely easy, thanks to cards that instantly convert them by withdrawing cash at any ATM. Still, we have come to this over time, through an evolution that has lasted years. As anyone can imagine, initially, there was no real market as there is today; initially, there was only BTC. The simplest way to convert it into fiat currency was to exchange it for cash physically. Bartering was not a very rational way to manage it, so soon, the first exchange platforms (exchanges) were born, allowing us to exchange even large volumes of cryptocurrencies easily.

LocalBitcoin

From the first moment, it seemed apparent that the easiest way to exchange cryptocurrencies was in person and that to build a "market" of this type (therefore based on a sort of barter), it was necessary to resort to the web. The success of the internet, not surprisingly, has also passed through services that allow the sale of goods or services between individuals.

With BTC, things went exactly like this; even today, there is a site called Localbitcoins (online since 2012), which connects those who buy and sell cryptocurrencies locally. However, through Localbitcoins (and other similar sites), supply and demand are limited to the meeting. They have a first approach, while the real currency exchange is managed in person, typically in cash. In large cities, it is not difficult to find someone who also wants to buy significant amounts of cryptocurrencies by paying for them with cash, but it is no less challenging to suffer from scam attempts in this way. Many people found themselves with thousands of euros of counterfeit money.

Therefore, it is always preferable to have due precautions when proceeding with this type of exchange and never take anything for granted. The risk of being scammed must always be considered. Although it may seem unsafe, this type of exchange is still very much in vogue today, especially since the job offer also moves through these channels. Many people around the world have Cryptocurrency to spend and would like to invest it in their projects.

It is not common to find advertisements on these platforms to be a baker. Still, there are numerous related translation jobs, the creation of websites and smartphone applications, and a vast number of job advertisements related to the blockchain. (issue a token, create a smart contract, write articles for specialized sites, etc.). All these testify to crypto technology's revolutionary door, around which blockchain was born much more than a simple market. A real economy was run with lots of jobs, university courses with secure professional outlets, and projects financed for millions of euros.

The existence of sites like Localbitcoins shows us how the "crypto-economy," contrary to its detractor's claim, is not based on nothing but rests instead on concrete foundations and is supported at different levels. It is frankly impossible to think that people who have already come into contact with this technology, who have understood how it works, and who already use it regularly can stop doing it in the next ten years. At the same time, it is not difficult to imagine that more and more people may decide to start using any of the hundreds of cryptocurrencies currently available on the market in a similar period.

The Escrows

If in any big city in the world, finding someone who wants to exchange cryptocurrencies is quite simple, things are not as easy in small towns. Despite this, I, who also live in a small town, was surprised to find a person less than 2km from me who wanted to sell 3BTC in 2016.

To be honest, that person was also the only one in the whole province, so it was a coincidence that he was right near my house. To all this, we must add that in many countries, banks are, understandably, reluctant to favor the movement of money towards cryptocurrencies and tend to block incoming and outgoing transfers connected to the accounts of some large exchange platforms. So how can you exchange cryptocurrencies even for significant amounts through the internet without risking taking the proverbial package? Simple, we use special services called "escrow." There are dozens of sites that allow you to do precisely this; the system is as simple as it is ingenious.

These sites are nothing more than a catalog of third parties who manage the transaction on behalf of all the parties involved; each of these users has a rating and requires a fee to carry out such a delicate task. The commission needed for each escrow varies according to the rating that the user has accumulated, as the rating reflects the user's reliability.

With this system, therefore, scams become extremely rare and challenging. Escrows tend not to act in bad faith since they are paid for their reliability, and their reputation is their livelihood. This system, of course, is not exactly the cheapest of all and probably not even the most comfortable way to exchange fiat currency for cryptocurrencies. However, it has been used by thousands of users who have testified to its quality and effectiveness for years.

Exchange Platforms

There are many reasons you may want to trade cryptocurrencies. There are also many different ways to do it. However, we need to make clear that there is a right way to satisfy every other need. Not taking this into account when dealing with cryptocurrencies can lead to unpleasant inconveniences. A prevalent mistake is that the function of an exchange platform (or exchange if you prefer) is to allow the conversion of different cryptocurrencies into other currencies or fiat currency.

In reality, this type of service was created to allow trading and not simply allow you to change your currencies. For example, imagine a lawyer who agrees to be also paid in Cryptocurrency; since only a few clients decide to pay him this way, the lawyer tends not to spend that money and eventually accumulates a tidy sum on his BTC address.

At some point, our lawyer will want to spend this sum, and perhaps instead of spending his coins as they are, he decides that the time has come to convert them into euros; what is the most comfortable way to do it? Well, just open an account on one of the largest and most reliable trading platforms on the market and transfer the BTCs to their address, at which point you place a sell order in euros, and that's it, right? Well, things won't necessarily turn out to be that simple. The moment our lawyer tries to transfer the sum just converted into euros to his current account, the account could be frozen because he didn't read the compliance policy.

Not all exchanges adhere to this type of protocol. It simply depends on the different rules that different countries apply to manage this type of market. In Italy, for example, opening an exchange requires compliance with very stringent regulations and is therefore not a simple (and even less economical) activity to start.

This set of rules (compliance) provides, among other things, the identification of users (which is why today, almost all platforms require the sending of user documents) and that the funds deposited are explicitly used for trading. Our lawyer was wrong in thinking he could exchange his BTC. Since his behavior is considered improper and expressly prohibited by the regulation of the platform, our lawyer found his account frozen.

This does not mean that it is not possible to use an exchange platform to change our BTC? The lawyer is just one example of the risks that a lazy person takes when not doing things with due attention, but there are numerous exchanges on the market, even among the largest, which do not have such strict rules.

The world of cryptocurrencies is refractory to the regulations imposed from above, hence the fact that users (including traders themselves) are forced to sacrifice their privacy to legitimately operate with their coins (since they have to submit their documents to exchange platforms for opening an account.) It's not exactly one of the most popular norms within the community; at a certain point, users on social networks, forums, and blogs began to tell each other that it would not be a bad idea to build a decentralized exchange.

After all, what else is an exchange platform but an updated register of all the exchanges made? The type of data processed through a blockchain, as long as a decentralized network of nodes guarantees its functioning. At this point, anyone can guess why there are at least a dozen platforms that offer precisely this service in the market. Users can transfer their coins to these platforms and trade like they currently do with large centralized exchanges. Where is the difference? In this way, they can do it anonymously and, in many cases, without paying commissions for every operation they make.

A recent innovation has also contributed to making this even easier to achieve, known as the "atomic swap," which allows users to use a smart contract to process an exchange of currencies between coins belonging to different chains. The smart contract essentially acts as a real escrow (thus protecting both parties involved) to send the coins to the relevant valid addresses. Suppose a user wants to buy ETH using their BTC. A smart contract will take its BTC, search for one or more users capable of satisfying the request at a price set by the user. As soon as possible, it will self-execute by paying the respective parts to the addresses each of them will have previously established.

Decentralized exchanges are one of the best examples of disintermediation's advantages, which, inevitably, also coincides with a drop in the costs incurred by the end-user. The cost reduction becomes an extraordinary incentive to convince more users to abandon centralized models in favor of decentralized ones. Hence the reason new technologies based on disintermediation and decentralization seem inevitably destined to win.

Nuggets to Note While Choosing a Cryptocurrency Exchange

Features

Platforms offering many features (margin trading, complex charts, and advanced order types) are advisable for very professional traders. This is because you will need to know how the crypto industry works to utilize these features. For beginner traders, the lesser the features of the exchange, the better.

Functionality

It doesn't matter whether you are a beginner, intermediate level, or expert trader - what matters is that you confirm the functionality of your platform before trading. Most importantly, you may want to consider if the exchange accepts your currency.

Fees

Every platform has a unique fee structure meant for different types of traders on their platform. You must check what the fee structure is on a cryptocurrency exchange platform before choosing it.

Privacy

It is indeed practically impossible for you to keep trading without anyone knowing who you are. Yet, you need to ensure a good level of privacy offered before you choose any cryptocurrency exchange.

Security

A side-effect of anonymity in the crypto world is that security is always vital when trading cryptocurrencies. You should assess all the same factors when selecting an exchange as you do with a crypto wallet. However, there is one significant difference. Exchange is designed for quick and simple transactions, which occasionally may compromise security.

Key Storage

A standard exchange will combine all user assets from the whole platform. Then, withdraw a considerable percentage and keep it in a cold wallet. That way, if the platform is attacked, the loss is minimal, if any.

Insurance

Indeed, cryptocurrencies are still very recent. Hence, a large part of the industry is unregulated. So, to a large extent, the responsibility of your insurance is in your own hands. Yet, some exchanges that adhere to government regulations provide insurance services for your funds. And a few others have 3rd party insurance packages for your crypto assets.

User Experience

This factor is divided into three parts:

1. As a beginner, you want to be confident that you are using an exchange with a basic layout and user interface. That way, you can successfully navigate through the exchange platform. An experienced trader will enjoy an advanced and sophisticated interface.

2. You should check what others have to say about the crypto exchange services. Check out their ratings to know if they will serve you well.

3. Check out their customer service.

How do they handle disputes? Are they always readily available?

Chapter 7

What You MUST Know Before Getting Started

Bitcoin trading provides an opportunity to earn returns on your money and diversify your investment portfolio. But before you begin trading, there are some basic things you need to know about Bitcoin investment.

Invest What You Can Afford to Lose

The truth about Bitcoin trading, given its volatility, is that nothing is ever guaranteed. Putting your retirement funds or life savings into a cryptocurrency investment is not recommended. Of course, it is unlikely that you'll have money that you don't mind losing. But the idea is to reduce how much you will be affected by lousy trading by using funds that will not affect you directly.

Do Not Get a Loan

This is similar to the first point. Although Bitcoin has come a long way from the early days of limited knowledge and widespread misinformation, the value is still quite volatile. Taking a loan to finance your Bitcoin investment is not a recommended move.

Do Your Research

Reading this book is a step in the right direction. But there are plenty of other things to learn as well if you want to become a good trader. You will need to monitor the news and follow the current happenings in the crypto world. You will also need to research exchanges and make an informed decision about any cryptocurrency platform you need to use. You will also need to have access to technical, analytic tools that make it easier to analyze and understand the market. In this final chapter of this book, we have included some resources that you will find valuable in your journey to becoming an expert Bitcoin investor.

Set Realistic Expectations

A common myth in the early days of Cryptocurrency was that it was a sure way to wealth. Trading Bitcoin is not the lottery of a money-doubling scheme. Don't expect to become a millionaire overnight from trading Bitcoin. You should set realistic expectations for yourself. When trading the market, don't be too greedy. Losses may happen once in a while. Know when to count your losses and exit the market.

Building your investment with Bitcoin takes a lot of time and patience. This is important if you intend to buy and hold Bitcoin and wait for prices to rise. If you follow this strategy, you must be patient enough to resist pressure from pundits and analysts. Sometimes your ability to block out the noise will make all the difference between whether you make a profit or loss in the long run.

So, how many coins should you buy?

The price of Bitcoin has grown high since its early days. This means you need a considerable sum of money to buy one unit of Bitcoin. Fortunately, you can buy less than one unit of Bitcoin, depending on how much you have. The number of coins you need to buy depends mainly on your investment strategy and the kinds of portfolio you intend to build.

With that said, there are some factors that you should consider in deciding how much your starting investment in Bitcoin should be. Let's go over five of these significant factors.

Your Risk Tolerance

Investing in Bitcoin is a risky venture. The market is quite volatile. While this means you can efficiently grow your investment, it also means you can lose everything if you make a terrible investment decision. You need to have this in mind before investing in Bitcoin. A basic rule of thumb is only to invest an amount of money in feeling comfortable losing in its entirety. So let's say you intend to invest $10,000; ask yourself if you will feel comfortable losing this entire sum in the future. Of course, losing any amount of money is not easy. But will you lose sleep over it? Many suicide cases have been reported following an investment loss. Determining your risk tolerance threshold will guide you to know how much you should invest. Even if you don't lose all your money, investors afraid to lose too much money because their life and future are tied to it cannot effectively take advantage of the market. Bringing your emotions into the decision-making process can potentially bring losses. Hence why you should keep your investment amount at a level that will not affect your judgment.

Determine Your Profit Tolerance

Funny question: "What would you do if you made $2 million with your $10,000 investment?". What happens if you lose all your money? Reflecting on this will also help you figure out what would happen in the event of a boom. This is a possibility with Bitcoin trading. You can make so much that you become too greedy and lose everything again. Imagine what happened to those who invested in Bitcoin back in 2017. Some of these investors become millionaires as a result of the boom. But not every one of them had a happy ending. Some investors who became overnight millionaires during the boom did not take their profit. They stayed back in the market to profit and lost it all when the market crashed in 2018.

The same rule still stands. Keep your investment at a level that a sudden boom will not affect your judgment. The key is to invest only when you feel emotionally detached from enough to make a sound judgment.

Timing

In the case of volatile assets like Bitcoin, timing is everything. The bitcoin market consists of several repeated rise and fall cycles. These cycles can last for a year or two. During these cycles, prices spike quickly, only to burst suddenly, leaving many investors high and dry. If there is anything you have to get right about investing in bitcoin, it is the timing. The timing also determines how much you should invest in bitcoin.

Typically, the media tend to make a lot of noise about bitcoin and other cryptocurrencies during a price surge. This gives you the impression that the time to buy is now and not anytime later. Before you decide on how much to invest, let the timing guide you.

Check the current cycles and the history of the market cycles. Is the market near an all-time high or approaching a low? The worst time to invest is when the market is nearing an all-time high. However, this is not to say you should only buy bitcoin when prices are low. There is no perfect time to buy Bitcoin. Whether prices are surging or dropping, what matters is that you understand the current position of the market before you get started and let it guide how much your initial investment will be.

Take Your Time

Don't succumb to the pressure and jump into the market right away without ensuring that is the amount you want to invest. If you give it enough time, you will likely change your mind after a while, especially when you notice changes in the market trends. Investing $5,000 may seem like a perfect idea now, but will you still feel the same way in, say, 3 or 6 months down the line. I always recommend that new investors take their time before deciding how much to invest. Don't jump into the market. Leave enough room for you to change your mind.

Several strategies can help you ease into the market. One simple trick is to break your investments into smaller chunks and invest them gradually over a given period. Progressive investment this way will help you understand the market and yourself better before you fully commit.

Another strategy is to invest gradually based on market cycles. For instance, if the market is near an all-time high right now, and you feel a bubble might be imminent, you can choose to reduce your initial investment. Let us consider an example of your original plan to invest 10,000 dollars in small chunks of $1,000. You can make your first investment $600 instead and then compensate for it with a more extensive sum once you feel the market has stabilized.

Diversify

You've probably heard the saying, "don't put all your eggs in one basket" before. This applies to every possible type of investment, including trading Bitcoin. To safeguard your investment, it is best to diversify your investment portfolio with different assets. For this, you can consider either correlated assets or uncorrelated assets.

For correlated assets, you can consider investing in other cryptocurrencies like ETH, XRP, or Litecoin. This way, you can consolidate your investment on multiple fronts. But a much better approach is to invest in assets that are not correlated to Bitcoin, such as gold, real estate, and stocks. These types of assets are not directly affected by the factors that affect the price of Bitcoin. Allocating your resources to any of these other assets will help secure your portfolio.

Chapter 8

Cryptocurrency Mining

What is Mining?

All of this requires enormous amounts of computing power, even though blockchain technology tries to allow anyone with the resources to 'mine' Bitcoin or other cryptocurrencies. "Heigh-ho, heigh-ho, it's off to work we go!" No, not that kind. This is our second misnomer and can be a bit confusing. Miners are not meaning anything; instead, they confirm transactions on the network and add them to the Blockchain. In return for this, they are automatically rewarded with free cryptocurrency by the Bitcoin software. They don't 'mine' it as such. Still, it's a reasonably good comparison to physically mining gold in that both require work, effort, and rarity to define their value. Bitcoin or gold can be automatically guaranteed their value just because the work has already been done.

Proof-of-work does not automatically and exclusively guarantee proof-of-success. Only once the rocks or the numbers have been crunched can the market decide whether the formula provides value. It's the same with all forms of asset, past, present, or future. Thankfully, the market has decided that Bitcoin does have value. Significant value at that, and a real future. Remember, it has been around 12 years, after all. All manner of naysayers have tried to discredit it, and Bitcoin just brushes them off. This is not a flash in the pan. It's not even a 'tech-bubble anymore. Bitcoin has proved itself to be a contender.

It helps to understand the mining process correctly, which is a little trickier to grasp right off the bat fully. Because, well, it genuinely seems a bit bonkers at first. But, rest assured, there are reasons for everything that Satoshi has done. Suppose we remember the work element of centuries-old money systems like the Rai stone or gold. The same principle applies to Bitcoin. Their value is determined partly because of the sheer amount of work gone into hew the stone or dig up the gold. In the same way, Bitcoin is deliberately tricky to 'mine' because the code forces miners to complete challenging mathematical problems to gain a chance of writing the following block to the Blockchain. This difficulty is intentional, giving it an ever-increasing value and helping to keep the network robust (safe). Not just anybody can do it because it takes serious resources, but there are many mining collectives made up of thousands of public individuals' computers, called mining pools. A consensus is reached among miners, and the first person or pool to complete the task correctly is rewarded in crypto.

Nobody knows who that is until several miners have effectively come up with the same answer, and thus the network, as a whole, has sufficiently verified all the transactions in the block. Effectively everyone is working together towards the same end. That means that the block is checked multiple times before it gets added to the Blockchain. In the case of Bitcoin, each block always takes ten minutes to solve. We are putting a file in the filing cabinet (Blockchain) every ten minutes to use our earlier analogy. The difficulty of the computational task is changed regularly, according to demand, to achieve that. This is another brilliant subtlety introduced by bitcoin. Bitcoin is always running the numbers and evolving accordingly, all by itself. Miners are rewarded in newly minted Bitcoin that the code distributes with each completed block. The block-reward since May 2020 has been

6.25 coins per block, which is a considerable amount. According to demand and worldwide mining capacity, the code cleverly alters the scarcity of Bitcoin and computational difficulty. It will take until the year 2040 to mine the last 2.5 million or so Bitcoins. The first 18.5 million or so have already been mined in the first twelve years.

As part of the economic/technology rules of Bitcoin, this reward halves approximately every four years or every 210,000 blocks. From 50 Bitcoins per block in 2009, they had three times to 6.25 in 2020. This makes the coins in circulation scarcer, and thus, the theory goes, more valuable. This process is called 'the Halving' or 'Halving,' and many cryptocurrencies operate in the same way. Rewards are different from other coins, and since October

2020, Ethereum miners now receive more in fees (gas) than they do in block rewards. That is due to the vast number of smart contracts running on their Blockchain, which has recently pushed prices sky-high. Horses for courses, though, Bitcoin sticks to what it's good at doing. Money. More on Smart Contracts and Ethereum in chapter 8.

One significant factor critical to the value is that the code automatically adjusts mining difficulty according to demand and market value. Sometimes, it takes less effort than others, depending on how many people are trying to solve it and the demands on the system. The beautiful code brings solid economic theory at every turn while simultaneously being one of the most innovative pieces of tech in our lifetime. There are others, don't get me wrong, like DNA editing or the internet itself. But Bitcoin is right up there.

Thus the Bitcoin blockchain is super secure and prevents problems like 'Double Spend,' where the owner of an electronic currency spends it twice. The robust and decentralized mining network verifies that it can only ever be spent once. Once it's hatched in a block, it can't be retracted or changed - ever. So it's not Bitcoin you have to worry about getting hacked; it's you, your email, a wallet, or a third party company or exchange you're using. And anything that's sitting on top of the Bitcoin blockchain itself. You still need to take care of those basics, all your passwords and 2FA (2-factor authentication), and always be on the lookout for phishing or worse.

As I have said, Bitcoin does have an Achilles heel. Power. The entire system of servers worldwide was, by late spring 2020, using an astonishing 7 gigawatts of electricity, or 64-terawatt hours (TWh) of power annually, twenty times that of Facebook's servers (5.1 TWh in 2019). That's as much as several countries' total consumption - for example, Portugal, Switzerland, Chile, Kuwait, or Ireland.

Horrific as that sounds, that's not the whole story. Most people don't realize how much the internet itself uses, with giant server farms all over the world now. It's no coincidence that many of these are neighbors of some of the world's largest fossil fuel power plants. Bitcoin represents 'only' around 1000th of the total energy used by the internet as a whole. Approximately 62 trillion spam messages are sent every year, requiring the use of 33bn kilowatt-hours (KWh) of electricity and causing around 20 million tonnes of CO_2e per year. Not a lot of people know that.

Importantly, much of this comes from renewable energy sources, such as geothermal in Iceland or excess hydroelectric power capacity in countries like China. Much of the Chinese power is already surplus to requirements, especially in the rainy season, and it has about the cheapest electricity in the world.

Add to that the fact that to run any payments system like a bank requires physical buildings, entire skyscrapers in major cities, staff driving to work every day, and other colossal running costs. Not to mention their server costs. It starts to make a bit more sense. Additionally, the likely progression is that technology will advance quickly enough so that the hardware will become faster, more and more energy-efficient as time goes on. Like renewable energy itself, there are challenges, but the future is undoubtedly electronic.

Crypto Mining

Crypto mining is a straight game in this digital era. Bitcoin was the primary decentralized currency, and it was introduced in early 2000. Cryptocurrency mining is a complicated procedure of verifying transactions and adding them to the Blockchain's public ledger. The Blockchain confirms all the transactions that have taken place to all networks. Blockchain is also accountable for releasing new bitcoins. The transactions carried out between two parties over a network are confirmed by miners. Miners utilize their hash power to verify and confirm all the transactions that have taken place over the networks. These transactions are then combined into blocks before they are added to the Blockchain. The blockchain records and stores all the details related to each transaction.

Miners use special software for mining cryptocurrency. The software connects your computer or laptop to other computers on a network to verify transactions and release new cryptocurrency units into circulation. Cryptocurrency miners run mining software on their computer systems to complete complex mathematical calculations for confirming the transaction. In turn, they receive cryptocurrency coins as rewards in return for their confirmation services. Cryptocurrency mining computers work like regular computers, except they run cryptocurrency software instead of operating systems. Cryptocurrency mining software is dedicated to the cryptographic algorithms involved in processing transactions, creating new blocks, and signing transactions. Mining hardware also plays a crucial role in the mining process. It performs the mathematical calculations required for verifying transactions and releasing cryptocurrencies.

There are Two Types of Cryptocurrency Mining Software:

1. Open-source Crypto mining software – This crypto mining software is open to everyone who wishes to download it from their website or other places on the internet. Open-source crypto mining software can be used by both individual users as well as businesses. They can configure the mining software according to needs and requirements.

2. Closed source Crypto mining software – This type of cryptocurrency mining software is not open to the public, but it is available for purchase by anyone who wishes to buy it. The closed source crypto mining software may not be free, but it has additional features that may give it an edge over other types of mining software.

Cryptocurrency miners can choose their hardware and configure it accordingly depending on their needs – GPU, CPU, Graphics cards, etc. Most GPU miners use either AMD or Nvidia-based graphic cards for crypto-coin mining. GPU mining is one of the most efficient and profitable ways of mining cryptocurrencies. As we all know, mining uses a lot of power, and that's why GPU mining is so popular because it costs much less than CPU or ASIC mining.

Cryptocurrency Mining Pools:

Mining pools are groups of cooperating miners who agree to share block rewards in proportion to their contributed mining hash power. Before a miner can begin mining Cryptocurrency, they need two things: a cryptocurrency wallet and hardware for mining. A cryptocurrency wallet allows you to store your digital currency so that you can make transactions with them anonymously without having to connect your name with your balance through the blockchain ledger. Some exchanges are handling crypto hardware wallets, and others are encouraging their users to manage them.

Each Cryptocurrency has its blockchain technology. Together they make up a distributed ledger called a blockchain that keeps track of all the transactions ever made on that particular network. For example, Bitcoin is the most popular Cryptocurrency ever created, and it is a part of what many people consider to be the cutting edge of technology today.

Cryptocurrency miners use special software to solve mathematical problems and verify transactions to get new tokens. They get paid directly from crypto mining pools or exchanges to solve these complex mathematical computations and confirm transactions. These transactions are later recorded in the Blockchain, which works as a public ledger. They get the coins of newly created coins in exchange for offering their computing power to maintain and confirm transactions on the blockchain network.

As more and more miners join a single mining pool, the chances of solving a block also increase, so do the payout per block. This is why every cryptocurrency mining pool is so competitive. The maximum reward for mining blocks on your own is when you hit 100% of the difficulty target or solve 2,147,483,647 DIFFICULTY (there are such numbers involved in crypto mining).

The Process of Mining

Cryptocurrency is intended to be secure, decentralized, and unalterable. Every transaction is scrambled and added to a block till some numbers of transactions have been verified.

When mining cryptocurrency, the miner has to collect current transactions into the blocks and crack a complicated puzzle. There are numerous bitcoin mining sites online. It is one of the most overriding ways to earn money these days. Cryptocurrency is cryptographic; that is to say, it uses encryption that permits coin generation and transaction confirmation control. Bitcoin mining for profit is highly competitive, so the miner has to be technical.

The Secrets to Mining Cryptocurrency

Decentralized currency is more popular than ever before. Coins can be used for different purposes: investing, trading, buying goods and services, or getting a small amount of interest when placed in a wallet or bank account. The crypto coins are not controlled by anyone else but the owner. A lot of new cryptocurrency coins have appeared on the market recently. Therefore, it's crucial to pick the best cryptocurrencies in terms of market situation and demand. Some believe that mining cryptocurrencies are the future of money, while others think it is just a thing to do during leisure time – like collecting stamps, but with much more potential for profit. If you are looking to mine for profit, you should consider what coins are the most profitable to mine.

Cryptocurrency mining is a principal activity.

Miners can simultaneously extract or mine many different cryptocurrencies, although there are some more lucrative ones than others. You may have heard of Bitcoin, Ethereum, Litecoin, and Dash – these are the most widely used coins for mining, and you can improve your chances of earning more with them than with other less popular ones. Mining multiple cryptocurrencies at the same time may improve your possibility of earning more money.

It is possible to mine alternative coins using the same equipment, but your profit per day will be lower. The dual mining feature, which is available on some mining software, may allow you to mine two different coins at the same time while allocating a specific percentage of resources to both. By considering the market price and mining difficulty, you can find out which coins are more profitable than others and improve your chances of making money.

Cryptocurrency trading is another way for miners to earn money. As a customer, you can exchange Bitcoins for USD or any other currency of your choice and vice versa. You can do this anywhere in the world without too many restrictions and limitations.

The Perfect Coins to Mine

The mining of bitcoin is not the perfect choice for new miners. Currently, Bitcoin mining is strictly for extensive scale activities. Feathercoins, Litecoins, and Dogecoins are Scrypt-based currencies that are sufficient money-saving plus for newbies. At the current estimation of Litecoin, there is a possibility of gaining from 50 pennies to 10 dollars per day using the customer-level mining hardware. Feathercoins and Dogecoins will return lesser benefits with comparable mining hardware, yet they are gaining more popularity daily.

The more people join the crypto coin surge, the harder it is to mine because you will need more expensive hardware to mine more coins. You will be forced to invest more in the mining hardware, or you will go for a less demanding coin. You need to think of running costs when you are mining. Some coin developers charge for their block reward to improve security; this may be unfavorable to you. The transaction fees usually are an essential component of the cryptocurrency mining profitability calculation. A lot of altcoins have low transaction fees, and they may become more advantageous in the future.

Alternative coins are increasingly picking up popularity.

If you happen to have 1GH/s of mining hardware, you are lucky because you can mine several alternative coins. The best thing is that there are many alternative coins, so it will continue to be profitable even if the difficulty rate increases. Most people are more interested in trading and investment than mining for their profit unless they have special hardware that will allow them to mine multiple currencies simultaneously and give them greater profits. Mining altcoins is an excellent way to get started with altcoin trading because they don't cost much. Mining altcoins can be a great way to start mining for pleasure or profit.

You should test the coin profitability and have some experience before going big on Crypto mining. Many miners believe that altcoin mining is the future, and some prefer to stick with more popular coins. Even though profitability might differ from coin to coin, it is recommended that you stick with older coins because they are also more stable. If you are a newcomer, every $100 in initial investment can bring $500-$1000 of profits in a month. Nowadays, there are scams everywhere around us – even in currency trading and investment.

The Advantages of Bitcoin Mining

No need to trust in a third party or middleman:

The number one advantage of cryptocurrency mining is that you don't have to rely on any financial institution or a third party because nobody will manage your money for you. Cryptocurrency is a decentralized digital currency that cannot be controlled by any government, organization, or centralized institution. Bitcoin and other digital currencies are a new phenomenon that was first introduced in 2009 by the mysterious person known as Satoshi Nakamoto. Cryptocurrencies are not bound by your location, language, or identity. You only need a computer system with Internet access and some skills – the rest will handle itself.

You get Free Bitcoin as a Reward

We are all aware that bitcoin transactions are accumulated into groups called blocks, and these blocks are confirmed roughly every ten minutes. The mining computers will try to solve a block through a series of equations, and the first computer to do it successfully will receive the block reward. Miners will also get all the transaction fees included in the block. So you can see that bitcoin mining will make a better passive income. The reward you got from mining can be sent to your wallet once you make your request.

1. Lesser Fees and Fast Transaction

In divergence from buying crypto, mining Bitcoin includes smaller fees (if you joined an excellent pool), and mining transactions are always faster than buying. In addition, you will be able to save from withdrawal and deposit fees when mining bitcoin.

2. Improving the Strength of the Security Network

The more miners contribute hash power to the network, the lesser the vulnerability. Cybercriminals and hackers will do everything possible to control good numbers of mining equipment instantaneously to interrupt the Bitcoin network. The more the miners, the more stable and secure the network will be.

3. Ability to Earn More Cryptocurrencies Using Your Hardware

You can mine multiple currencies depending on your hardware quality, cost of electricity, and the current price of Bitcoin. There are different profitable rates of bitcoin mining. On the other hand, you can switch to other currency pairs depending on what you feel is beneficial.

4. Long Term Investment

Cryptocurrencies are likely to grow in time – it's a long-term investment, but with high profits if you do it right. As the price of digital currencies goes up, mining will become more competitive and less profitable. However, the rewards will increase if you choose a more expensive currency than mine. It's all up to you how much money you're willing to spend on mining and what coins you want to mine for the future.

How Can You Make Money Offline with Cryptocurrency Mining?

You can make your profit offline with cryptocurrency mining in many ways; it depends only on your creativity and willingness to deal with complicated technologies and different software solutions for individual tasks.

Here are Some of the Ways You Can Do It:

1. You can use Cryptocurrency to buy real estate or other physical property. Many people have already started to realize that this is a great investment opportunity in their local markets. Buying a house or property with bitcoin can be a great way to get back into the market if you don't want to mine any longer.
2. You could invest in renewable energy sources and start mining Cryptocurrency for profit as a side activity, just like buying and selling cryptocurrencies in your spare time on the side, just for fun.
3. You can sell Cryptocurrency for fiat. This is the best option if you want to cash out Cryptocurrency for real money or use it for any other means.

4. Online business is another opportunity you could explore. Cryptocurrency has opened the doors to many possibilities that will allow you to make money online. Selling ebooks, courses, and any other digital product is an excellent way to raise some funds to invest back into mining equipment/hardware so that you can make even more profit. You can also use your earnings to buy cryptocurrencies and hold them until their price rises so that your investment will pay off in the long run, just like in any other high-yield investment opportunity.

What Secrets Do You Wish to Learn About Cryptocurrency Mining?

Cryptocurrency mining is not as easy as it seems. If you are a newbie, there are lots of things that may confuse you. You need time to learn and understand everything that's going on in the mining industry and how Cryptocurrency works, but there are some basics you can follow right away:

1. Do your research – ask questions, read some books and articles or watch videos on Youtube and Reddit.
2. Start with smaller cryptocurrencies first – go for those with lower prices so that you won't lose a lot of money if something goes wrong.
3. Try to go for renewable energy sources if you can, because it will save you a lot of money in the long term.

4. Don't forget about the mining equipment itself – try to find satisfactory hardware that will work best for your requirements, and remember to buy an effective cooling solution for your equipment.

5. Plug in all devices only when necessary to stay focused and avoid accidents/errors.

But if you like technology and dealing with different software solutions, then cryptocurrency mining can be your passion that will bring additional income on the side.

Chapter 9

Different Investment Strategies

Bitcoin investors earn income with the difference of the buy or sell price. It's like investing in a property: you buy for a fee and hope to be able to sell it later for a higher price. The difference is your profit.

Many new stakeholders believe that buying bitcoin, holding it for a while, and selling it will earn income. However, it turns out that income is not fixed, predictable or stable. It may be that you buy Bitcoin, hold it for 100 days, and in the end, you lose money. In the end, your profit will always depend on purchasing at a lower price and selling one at a higher price, which is not predictable.

Some users arrive with the idea that bitcoin would function as a savings account: you deposit the money and then just go back to redeem the earnings. However, they do not understand that it is necessary to buy Cryptocurrency after depositing in a broker. In addition, after buying, at some point, you will need to sell to make real ones again. In other words, investing in Bitcoin and making profits comes down to:

Buy Cryptocurrency with real money.

- Expect to appreciate it.
- Sell the Cryptocurrency, turning it into reality again.
- Price changes and volatility

Bitcoin is often highlighted in the mainstream media during periods of high appreciation. This news attracts many new users to become investors, who buy in periods when the currency is "up there." However, it turns out that the natural movement after a significant recovery is a fall. In this way, new investors who bought during the peak period may be discredited with investments in cryptocurrencies when experiencing a possible loss right from their first experience.

Dealing with this is vital before we talk about any bitcoin price perspective. After all, you need to understand the minimum market movements and why bitcoin values or devalues.

First, it needs to be clear to you that bitcoin is brutally volatile. It means that the variations can be high and sudden, with fluctuations in short periods. One of the tremendous challenges for those who follow the market is to predict these movements. Although there are analysis techniques for this, such as those carried out, the only certainty is volatility. It's because?

The most accepted idea by experts is that, even though bitcoin has already gained a global scale, there is still a lot of concentration in the hands of large investors, who are called Whales. When these investors sell or buy a lot, the impact on the market can be incredible.

But what explains the variations in the price of bitcoin besides these cases of large transactions? The same explains the essence of any asset, product, or service price changes: supply and demand.

A broader discussion would fit into what generates bitcoin supply and demand. Many experts consider the market to be still new to reach all possible conclusions. Some events in the traditional financial market have already been shown to impact bitcoin, both for good and bad. But as it is a global currency traded in a market that does not stop in any country in the world, a cause and consequence analysis is practically impossible.

One of the unique beliefs of experts and scholars in this market is that, over time, as Bitcoin increases its capillarity in society and is adopted by more people, the trend is less volatile.

In the meantime, the best you can do is to mitigate your risks by making gradual investments and following the market. It is essential to distribute your purchases and sales over time and schedule Limit or Stop orders to control your losses and gains.

Learn now and choose the strategy that best suits your profile.

Arbitration

Practiced since the beginning of the maritime trade by merchants who sold silk from China in the port of Venice, the Arbitration consists of buying a product for a low price in one place and selling it at a higher price in another. Cryptocurrency investors worldwide take advantage of differences in buying and selling values between exchanges to profit, which can be a valuable practice, especially during times of price volatility. In this section, understand what it is, how it works, and why practice arbitration.

The simplest way to perform Arbitration is for the investor to transfer his cryptocurrencies from one exchange to another. Identifying an opportunity to buy at a low price and sell at a higher price, just make the transfer from the cheapest exchange. However, this activity requires a lot of attention, as price changes can be swift. Thus, the investor must monitor the price on the exchanges in which he arbitrates almost constantly.

Sometimes transactions can take a long time to complete, and when the money arrives at the other broker, the profit has either run out or decreased. So it is good to keep in mind the average speed of the brokers. For example, we always send our withdrawal requests with high priority. Some investors also do Arbitration with the help of robots, but this requires more study and programming knowledge.

The volatility of cryptocurrencies is precisely one of the main reasons that make them attractive for arbitrage, as it allows them to make good profits from the daily variations. Furthermore, the diversity of existing altcoins also allows to make considerable gains with the different conversion rates, both concerning traditional currencies (Real, Dollar) with Bitcoin. Another great advantage of arbitrage with cryptocurrencies is a large number of exchanges between Brazil and abroad, increasing the chances of gain.

Arbitration is an investment with a risk of loss. So, before practicing, that maxim is worth it: study well, read articles, books, and everything you can; after all, the more knowledge, the lower the chances of risk and the greater the chances of gain.

You need to trust the exchanges you trade with well. A risk worthy of attention is the need to leave the amount for arbitrage in the broker's portfolio. Fortunately, you can rest assured to have insurance for your reservations in the (doubtful) case that we suffer a hacker attack. The difference between the fees charged by the brokerage firms may seem small to the "naked eye," but as arbitrage usually requires large amounts, it can be just the difference between profit and loss.

For example, problems can always happen; for example, an exchange may have few resources available in the hot wallet on a busy day. Therefore, it is essential to have exchanges that understand what arbitrage is and the main points to know how to help you.

Hodl

Whether in the traditional stock market or the world of cryptocurrencies, each investor has their strategies. Like Warren Buffet - recognized worldwide as the most successful investor in the world - prefer to buy their assets and hold them indefinitely or for a considerable period. Among crypto-investors, this tactic is called "HODL" (check out its curious origin below) and consists of buying cryptocurrencies and keeping them for long periods, sometimes for years, for the most diverse reasons. This section understands what it is, how it works, and why to practice the "HODL" strategy.

The origin of this name is quite curious. After Bitcoin hit a € 1,000 high in December 2013, many investors decided to sell their reserves. With the increase in supply, the price fell, driving sales even more, and so on. A Japanese investor decided not to make any sales to save the coins in the belief of an even greater appreciation in the future. When writing an energetic post on the internet, declaring to the community his intention to hold, he got confused and wrote: "I AM HOLDING" instead of "I am Holding" (I am saving). It didn't take long for his caricature mistake to become a fever on the internet and, since then, the practice has been called HODL.

Why the holder? As a general rule, before any investment - be it in cryptocurrencies, stocks, or a real estate venture -, keep your potential in mind. So, before investing in a cryptocurrency, know its proposal, its structure, and its perspectives. This is the basic principle of fundamentalist analysis: what is based on solid foundations tends to grow and appreciate.

That said, holding cryptocurrencies is a strategy for those who understand its potential and the proposed digital revolution. Year after year, we have seen an increasing number of payment methods, stores, and services embracing the idea and using them. The holders see this move as a sign that digital currencies will be earlier large-scale use of what is expected and, therefore, it is natural that it is valued fairly. As they do not want to be left behind, they take advantage of this initial moment to invest before they are too expensive.

Not only for that reason, but it is also held. Especially in the case of Bitcoin, there is a historical upward trend that is repeated, creating a pattern. That is why, even in a bearish moment, as the current one, many investors are optimistic about the future. This is precisely when many holders take the opportunity to invest, aiming for the next high. It is the classic catchphrase, "buy low and sell high," even for years. After all, Bitcoin doesn't have to be a short-term investment! Using hold, investors who bought Bitcoin in 2016, valued at € 500, and sold it at 2017 high, at € 19,000, made a profit of 37,000%. Imagine those who bought at € 198, at the historic high of 2013, and decided to hold on for the entire period.

Many investors use mathematical and traditional financial market tools to interpret this history and make future value projections: technical analysis. However, contrary to what one might think, it is not antagonistic to fundamentalist analysis; both are often combined to build a Hold strategy.

You don't necessarily need to master the technical and fundamental analysis tools to hold. If you are not a professional investor, let alone have time to follow the daily fluctuations of this very volatile market, buy and hold can be the ideal strategy! But remember: never invest without doing a prior analysis.

Trade

Any purchase or sale can be considered a trade. But the term is commonly used to name the strategy of constantly taking advantage of price variations to buy at a lower price and sell at a higher price.

Day Trading

It is a short-term investment strategy. As the name says: you follow the market daily to make purchases and sales, taking advantage of the fluctuations that happen on the same day. When opting for Day Trade, you should be aware that you tend to profit very little from operations, as variations within the same day tend to be very small. So, even if it's a short-term strategy, higher returns can come if you repeat it for several days.

Like any other Trade strategy, you must know a little bit of visual analysis to predict with greater assertiveness the following movements. It is also essential to understand that this strategy requires more dedicated time, as you will need to keep an eye on the market within 24 hours).

Swing Trading

The logic of swing trading is the same as that of Day Trading, differing by the time window used to make trades. While in Day Trading, this time is 24 hours. That of Swing Trading can be days, weeks, or even months.

While in Day Trading, you will achieve a maximum yield of 1% to 3%, in Swing Trading, these gains tend to be much more remarkable, as you get an accumulation of fluctuations.

A fundamental part of this strategy is to program limit or stop orders. This way, you can set a target buy or sell price and guarantee that you will take advantage of volatility. It is also interesting to know graphic analysis to understand trends in future movements.

As an intermediary in transactions, a broker has custody over clients' assets. In other words, just like in a bank, you keep your money on company property, trusting that whenever you need it, you can transfer it or withdraw it as you wish.

What to Evaluate in a Brokerage House (Exchange)

- Confirm the company's existence: search for the CNPJ, check the location and corporate structure. Check LinkedIn to see if she has actual employees and who the directors are. Check if they are serious people with relevant professional history. See what they say on the "About" or "Who we are" page on its website.

- Find out about liquidity and volume: specialized sites. On these sites, you must consider the relevance of the broker and whether it will be able to make its assets available as soon as you request it.

- Beware of income promises: be wary of companies that promise earnings. Bitcoin is a volatile currency, and it is impossible to predict the currency's appreciation or devaluation. Profits must be obtained exclusively from the trading strategy you define.

- Transaction deadlines: search for deadlines for deposits and withdrawals in reais & cryptocurrencies. Within bank hours, they take up to 15 minutes. In addition, you can request a withdrawal at any time.

- Security: check if the exchange has protection against intrusions, in addition to 2-Factor Authentication (2FA) and Account Validation that guarantee even more security for your trades.

Escape the Pyramids

The logic of this type of fraud is simple: you give money in exchange for promises of earnings while advertising to more people to join the same business. While new people are coming in and putting money in, the company's commitment is fulfilled. After all, there is cash flow that can be used to pay previous users. However, it is no longer sustainable, as the promised gains do not find space in the reality of any market. The payment made by the new users at the entrance is used to pay the previous ones, but at some point, the entry of new ones is not enough to pay the old ones.

Investing for the Long Term

It is important to understand that there is no "best" strategy for investing in Cryptocurrency. Every investor must make their own educated decisions about how long they are willing to invest and the level of risk they are comfortable with. However, some strategies might be more suited for specific investors than others. For example, long-term holders are typically comfortable waiting out the market and not worrying too much about day-to-day movements in prices. Investors who engage in this strategy should invest in bitcoin or another cryptocurrency that has a fundamental purpose outside of being a currency; Ethereum and Litecoin would be two examples of this type of currency.

Strategies for long-term investing includes:

1. Always invest money you're okay with losing

This is a general rule for investing that can not be applied to every investment- specifically, Cryptocurrency. However, it still applies to most investments in diversifying your money and making sure you are not overinvesting in one particular asset.

2. Time horizon matters

Investors with a longer time frame tend to make better gains because they have more opportunities for capital appreciation and less risk. Additionally, there is a chance their investments will recover from any losses made during downturns caused by short-term market prices.

3. Risk matters

Risk is inevitable, and the more you put in, the more likely you are to lose your money. Knowing how much risk you are willing to take or want to incur is crucial in making the right decisions on buying and selling.

4. Never invest all of your money in one asset

This is a general rule for investing that can not be applied to every investment. In terms of diversifying your money and making sure you are not overinvesting in one particular asset.

5. Do not invest in something that you do not understand

There are plenty of investments out there that most Americans know little or nothing about, and they likely don't realize how much they do not know. The best rule of thumb is, to be honest with yourself and make sure you truly understand the risks, rewards, and mechanics before investing your hard-earned money in something unknown.

6. Do your research

There is no one way to make money, but you have to know how things work if you want them to work for you. Therefore, you should always research whatever investment you are making before putting your money into it, especially if a third party recommends it.

7. Make sure the investment makes sense

There are many potential investments out there that look very good on paper, but they don't make sense regarding the real-world application. So ultimately, you need to carefully compare the potential investment with the real world before you do anything else. Otherwise, it will be too late when something comes along and exposes the project as a scam.

8. Know how to manage an investment property

It's essential to understand how you will invest your money to make sure your expectations are realistic. Without a proper strategy, you could wind up losing money or making unreasonable amounts of it. Of course, it's easy to over-think and think about everything else before you do anything, but it is essential to clearly define what you want and follow through with your plans once the investment is made.

9. Know how much risk you are willing to take

Risk is inevitable, and the more you put in, the more likely you will lose your money because of bad luck or market movements. Knowing how much risk you are willing to take or want to incur is crucial in making the right decisions on buying and selling.

10. Never invest all of your money in one asset

This is a general rule for investing that can not be applied to every investment. In terms of diversifying your money and making sure you are not overinvesting in one particular asset.

11. Do not invest in something that you do not understand

There are plenty of investments out there that most Americans know little or nothing about, and they likely don't realize how much they do not know.

Investing for the Short Term

Short-term holders are typically more risk-tolerant. They do not want to invest in a currency that has the potential to lose value over time. In this case, investors might be better off investing in more liquid assets such as cash or ETFs, such as the Bitcoin Investment Trust (OTC: GBTC) or ProShares Short Bitcoin ETF (OTC: GBTC). Short-term holders usually look for cryptocurrencies that hold a lot of utility and store a good amount of value. Stablecoins would be an excellent example of this type of investment, as they allow people to hold and trade their Cryptocurrency at any time and any place.

Strategies for short-term investing includes:

1. Investing in cryptocurrencies-Gold or silver may have been good long-term investments last year, but cryptocurrencies are better.

2. Investing in crypto merchants-There is a list of four startups backed by venture capital firms, including Andreessen Horowitz and Union Square Ventures. They now accept payment in bitcoin instead of dollars.

3. Investing in mining equipment-Mining rigs that were once priced at a few hundred dollars apiece can be found for as little as $100 on Amazon with free Prime shipping thanks to the rise of Bitcoin's popularity

4. Exchange-traded funds investing

5. Investing in ICOs-Initial coin offerings, or ICOs as they are popularly called, are a way for startups spread over the world to fund their operations. The projects run by these startups use cryptocurrencies to raise money and get the tokens listed on exchanges for sale and trade. This is how these coins become investable.

6. Investing in Bitcoin futures-Bitcoin futures will only allow investors to speculate on the future price of bitcoin and not trade directly with it.

7. Investing short term in your own country's currency like the dollar or yen

8. Investing in other currencies, especially if you live in Argentina, where they offer a special Bitcoin bond that pays out when bitcoin goes above certain valuation levels

9. Investing in cryptocurrency mining equipment: You can also profit by buying and selling the equipment itself, but its price is already very high.

10. Investing in long term cryptocurrency storage

11. Investing in app coins-Many projects are still trying to figure out how to use blockchain technology to incentivize people to use their apps like Steemit or Brave. These app coins are used as rewards for anyone who uses the apps, and you can buy more if you want to increase your rewards.

12. Investing in new business models that use cryptocurrencies as part of their system like having your money managed by a hedge fund with higher returns but risks too

13. Investing in coin exchanges-Some of these exchanges allow you to buy and sell coins at different prices that are dependent on the supply and demand of the coin

14. Investing in a token sale-Here is a guide to how you can safely determine whether it is safe or not to invest in an ICO (Initial Coin Offering)

A cryptocurrency is a digital asset designed to work as a medium of exchange that uses strong cryptography to secure its transactions, control the creation of additional units, and verify the transfer of assets. Cryptocurrencies use decentralized control as opposed to centralized electronic money and central banking systems. Cryptocurrency markets are open to all investors around the world. By using cryptocurrencies, you can diversify your portfolio and have a chance to get rich.

The profit is directly proportional to the market cap of the currency. So, for example, if a particular cryptocurrency has a price of $100 and it is the fourth-largest Cryptocurrency in terms of market cap, it will be worth more than if it was the third in terms of market cap. So, in this case, if you buy one unit of that coin, you will receive four units of value that you can sell at any time in the future at a higher price.

Leveraging

Leveraging, or "parking," is when you invest in a high-risk asset with the understanding that you will not lose the amount you invested. For example, if you bought $1,000 worth of a cryptocurrency that doubled in value within one month, then your investment would be worth $2,000. However, if Cryptocurrency's price fell by 10% during that same time frame, it would only be worth $1,900. Therefore, instead of losing 20% of your investment (or $200), you would only lose 10%.

Another way to leverage is to invest in Cryptocurrency through a bitcoin and altcoin margin trading platform. This type of contract allows you to borrow money from the broker to increase your potential profit margin. For example, suppose that you would like to purchase $1,000 worth of Ethereum at $200 per Ether; however, your account does not have enough funds. You can open a short position on the platform by borrowing another $900 from your broker and using that money to purchase an ETH/USD contract (which will be worth 1 ETH once you close your position). Before taking this trade, you must understand how margin trading works.

For example, consider the following situation. Suppose that you open a short position, get $900 borrowed, and purchase an ETH/USD contract. If the price of ETH falls to $160 per Ether, then your total loss will be $1,000 (plus any interest lost on your margin account). However, if the price rises to $220 per Ether before you close your position (and you decide not to close at that price), then your overall profit will be the difference between what you initially purchased ($1,000) and what you sold it for ($1,900). On a margin trade, this would also mean that you would have to pay interest on your "loan" of $900 each day; this interest is known as the financing rate.

The takeaway message from this example is that leverage and margin trading are both high-risk strategies, as they often require more money than you originally intended to invest. It is essential to understand that leverage magnifies losses during periods of market volatility and generally does not improve profitability over time. Several studies are suggesting that leverage may harm your portfolio's overall long-term performance. Nevertheless, even when used properly, leverage can be a powerful tool for accumulating gains over time.

Compound Interest

This concept is one of the most powerful and useful ideas in all of finance. It explains why compounded returns are so much more profitable than simple returns. Compound interest is simply the growth of an amount that has already been received or invested over time. For example, if you start with $1 and invest it at a 3% annual rate for 10 years with no drops in value, then after 10 years your total money will be $2.10 ($1 x (1 + 3/100)) times ten years later it is also $2.10 times (1 + 3/100), or $2.90 ($2.10 x (1 + 3/100)).

Compound Returns

Traders use this term to describe the profit earned from investing over time rather than receiving a one-time payment. For example, suppose that you invested $1,000 in a cryptocurrency with a 10% annual gain, and it increases to $2,000 after ten years. Thus, your total investment has grown to $3,000 with no reinvestment of money into Cryptocurrency. This growth in wealth would be called compounding interest because the growth rate came from both the initial investment and reinvesting profits into it.

Compound returns are expressed as exponential, meaning that the growth rate is proportional to the amount invested. For example, suppose that you invested $1, and it grew by 10% per year over ten years. Your investment would compound at a rate of $(1 + .10)10 = 1.051010 = 2.2349792892$ x $0.01 = $2,245. The takeaway message here is simple: if you invest money into something that grows at a constant rate over time, then your money will start to work for you rather than vice versa.

One of the most important lessons to learn from this article is differentiating between simple interest and compound interest. Many people think that compound returns are a form of "interest" or "interest rate," but these terms are used interchangeably for exponential growth. The difference between simple and compound returns is often not understood, and in some cases, it is not even considered by investors.

The math behind compounding is also fundamental; understanding the rule of 72 will teach you everything you need to know about how money grows at a constant rate over time and how many years it will take to double your investment. In large part, this concept was inspired by my introduction to leverage in trading and investing.

Compounding is an essential concept in trading and investing because it allows you to have your money work for you. But, compound returns are not the same as simple returns. A simple return, or interest rate, cannot be used to calculate compound gains over time. This can be confusing for some investors. Here is a table that helps clarify this issue:

How to Use The Leverage

1. Get a margin account.
2. Find the leverage you need to buy at a price you're comfortable with.
3. Buy.
4. Repeat steps 2 and 3 until you get out of the trade, get stopped out, or cash out by buying back the position of your original margin account value (margin accounts can be used in both ways).
5. Calculate commissions like loss and profit to determine your overall profit or loss from buying on

margin and selling on leverage (if you choose to sell on leverage before buying back your position).

6. Evaluate your overall profit or loss and determine if you should buy on margin again (the margin buying and selling allow investors to realize returns in bullish and bearish market conditions, respectively).

7. Repeat until you've achieved your profitability objective or stopped trading due to a bad run.

I like using leverage because it gives me an edge over my competition. Leverage allows me to make more money when I'm right and cut my losses when I'm wrong. Anyone can become a profitable trader with enough practice by using leverage properly (expert traders use leverage extremely effectively). Especially with the use of proper risk management techniques, the benefits of leveraged speculation are undeniable. With that being said, it's imperative to recognize that leverage will work both for and against you.

Leverage can work against you by increasing your losses. And there are a few ways this can happen. Firstly, leverage will magnify your profits and losses (this isn't bad when using proper risk management techniques, as I will show you). Additionally, it's possible to leverage may work against you by increasing the probability of a catastrophic event (such as bankruptcy). Traders who lose too much money without limits or position limits in place will most likely go bankrupt due to adverse market conditions. When traders face bankruptcy, they begin to lose trades to get out of the red, putting them in even more danger. This can be avoided by having adequate limits or position limits set in place for each trader.

The Best Investment Strategy Includes:

1. Curtailing the riskiest investment to heighten the success of profit-making opportunities
2. Assimilating new knowledge and resources into the portfolio
3. Reducing the amount of market volatility as much as possible
4. Recognizing when to get out of a trade and minimize risk
5. Maximizing investment growth while incorporating an element of opportunity cost in any decision-making process
6. Calculating return on investment for each cycle of capital to determine where investments should be made
7. Making decisions based on what is best for each unique situation, not necessarily what is best for others or even yourself in different situations.

And while researching new and innovative ways to grow investment portfolios, it is often wise to look into anything outside the traditional stock market. For example, the cryptocurrency market is still in its infancy but increasing as more people become familiar with the technology that powers the decentralized network of transactions across a blockchain ledger.

The digital asset itself can sometimes be described as a virtual token that can exist across an entire decentralized global network, allowing it to be exchanged between anonymous parties without the need for intermediary financial institutions or central banks.

The Benefits of this Type of Digital Asset Include:

1. No central authority to regulate the currency or govern its operations
2. Transactions can be made securely and privately without any reliance on a third party
3. High speed and low transaction fees
4. Complete privacy and anonymity for users, even when transacting with other users outside the network (so-called "darknet"). Don't worry, you're still on the internet!
5. Transferring currency between different countries is easy because it doesn't rely on a third party to do the transaction between two parties as opposed to traditional banking networks that are primarily centralized

6. Enabling a new class of entirely decentralized applications (dApps) that are free from centralized points of failure

7. Coin creation is decentralized and allows for the elimination of inflation in the system

8. "Initial coin offering" (ICO) which is a new method to access and invest in the cryptocurrency market without being bound by a financial institution or regulatory bodies along with its associated risks

So, what exactly can you do with this new financial instrument? There are only two basic ways to interact with them: Investing in them to gain profits or spending them to gain value. As it stands now, you can only do one thing with most crypto assets, but there is always room for expansion.

While the fund may complement a traditional investment portfolio, it isn't expected to replace it. Instead, the fund will be a bridge between conventional investment instruments and cryptocurrency markets. It will provide an additional, fundamental resource of capital for investing in cryptocurrency assets without creating or requiring the involvement of a third-party intermediary such as a bank, broker, or financial advisor.

In terms of the actual market, there is an incredible amount of things that one can do. The cryptocurrency market is a multi-billion dollar economy still in its infancy, with a rapidly growing user base and new investment strategies being created every day.

The most common way to participate in such an environment would be to purchase cryptocurrencies directly on an exchange through a fiat-to-crypto pair. That means you would have to deposit U.S. dollars into your account on the exchange and then buy one or more cryptocurrencies directly from your account balance. Alternatively, you can buy by using other cryptocurrencies like Bitcoin to facilitate the transaction process at hand (fiat/crypto pair). However, this comes with significant risks, including:

1. High fees associated with transferring fiat directly to cryptocurrency markets
2. Lack of liquidity and ability to quickly purchase and sell a currency pair to maintain desired rate changes
3. Lack of transparency and liquidity in the market, which allows for manipulation of rates between the fiat currency pair and cryptocurrencies by others
4. Limited regulation in the exchange itself makes it inherently high risk, especially when dealing in unregulated markets like darknets
5. Digital asset prices fluctuating with no way to accurately track ownership of a specific market value when there is no intrinsic value to a digital asset beyond what is determined by supply, demand, and volume of trades
6. A large amount of risk associated with its market value for the average investor

7. Risk of cybercrime and hacking attacks on exchange platforms

While there are many applications in the cryptocurrency market alone (both private and public), many other digital assets are used for stocks, bonds, commodities, real estate, and more. In addition, you can also use crypto assets as a way to back up traditional investment portfolios through so-called "collateralized virtual currency" (aka Blockchain-based assurance agreements). Essentially, you would receive a portion of your principal from a conventional investment portfolio to exchange collateralized virtual currency assets. These asset holdings would then be subject to the same rules that apply to other traditional investments such as mutual funds or retirement portfolios. A significant benefit of these instruments is that they can hedge against the risk of traditional investment portfolios. By backing up traditional investment portfolios with crypto assets instead of fiat currency, you can enjoy lower volatility and downside risk while still maintaining a stable base of capital and exposure to the overall growth potential of the cryptocurrency market.

Another emerging security in this space is the decentralized autonomous organization, or "dapp." A dapp is similar to a business entity that uses special rules regarding ownership, capital allocation, and more. However, they are fully autonomous with no management team behind them; they often have open-source codebases that focus on transparency over secrecy. The primary goal of a dapp is to provide a more completely privacy-centric digital financial world, free from the restrictions and obligations imposed by centralized institutions.

These strategic directions have not gone unnoticed by the cryptocurrency community, with more than 20 projects explicitly created with Dapps in mind.

The first to emerge was Decodex on Jan 4th, 2017, designed to be the world's first decentralized digital asset index fund management platform. It allows for easy access to more than 10,000 digital assets using their unique DecodexCoin token (DDX). In addition, it uses smart contracts for automated investment management decisions similar to those built into Ethereum's native currency ERC20.

How Can You Profit from Investing in Cryptocurrencies?

Cryptocurrencies are a new form of money and payment system that emerged from the need to have digital cash. Cryptocurrency allows people to transfer value without an intermediary, such as a bank or government. Many cryptocurrencies, such as Bitcoin (BTC), were completely anonymous and decentralized to be controlled by any one party. Cryptocurrencies are typically stored in wallets that use encryption techniques to make digital transactions anonymous.

Instead of relying on central banks or other third parties, cryptocurrencies work by generating cryptographic hashes using CPU power from many different sources worldwide combined in a process known as mining. Mining is the process of verifying transactions and adding them to the Blockchain or the public ledger for a cryptocurrency. Once verified, these transactions are publicly recorded in a ledger that cannot be manipulated or changed without consensus from the network majority.

Of all of the different types of cryptocurrencies, one of the most popular is Bitcoin.

The value of Bitcoin skyrocketed in 2017, opening up a whole new world of investment opportunities. This has caused many investors to wonder how they can invest in Bitcoins without paying full value. Fortunately, there are now several ways in which you can invest in Bitcoins without having to buy them outright.

Going through an exchange can be one of the most popular options for investing in Bitcoin. Exchanges are essentially marketplaces where cryptocurrencies such as Bitcoin are bought and sold. Mt Gox was the first cryptocurrency exchange based on blockchain technology launched in 2011. As more and more investors became interested in cryptocurrencies, exchanges have started popping up worldwide.

Some new exchanges offer traders the option to trade fiat currency for cryptocurrencies which can be a great way to get involved without paying full value for a Bitcoin! Other websites allow you to trade one Cryptocurrency for another (crypto-to-crypto trading).

Many exchanges that allow you to trade fiat currency for Bitcoin offer leverage. This means that you can trade using much smaller amounts of money. For example, if you only had $200 to invest in Bitcoins, most exchanges would let you use this $200 even if the price of a single coin was $6,000. When trading with leverage, always remember that the higher the potential returns are because there is also a higher risk of losing your money if something goes wrong.

As with any type of investment, there is always risk involved when trading on leverage. However, as long as you are comfortable with the risks involved, leverage makes it possible to invest in cryptocurrencies using smaller amounts of money. Another option for investing in cryptocurrencies is through crowdfunding platforms. Crowdfunding platforms connect investors and entrepreneurs who are looking to get funded for their projects. Popular crowdfunding platforms that also support Bitcoin include Kickstarter and Patreon. This is also a great way of getting in on the ground floor of new projects and cryptocurrencies before they become mainstream.

Chapter 10

How To Choose A Crypto That Will Appreciate In Value

Different Parameters to Consider When Choosing a Cryptocurrency to Invest in

Cryptocurrency for investment is the hot new thing. But it's not as easy as just throwing money at the next crypto-coin that hits the market and hoping for immense returns. There are a lot of different factors to consider. That's why we've put together this post to introduce Cryptocurrency, complete with a breakdown of what they are, how they work, and why you should care about them. The parameters you must look at before choosing a cryptocurrency for investing includes:

1. What geographic markets the Cryptocurrency is being targeted at, and what regulatory hurdles need to be

overcome to be accepted in these markets- Cryptocurrency has to be targeted at a location with lots of people that are already using cryptocurrencies in their daily lives

2. The team behind the Cryptocurrency, with a track record of the experience and staying power to take it through adoption hurdles

3. The technology behind the currency and how much effort is being put into making it secure against threats such as hackers' zero-day attacks or government censorship

4. A community of users that will be able to support mass adoption and improve the services around your Cryptocurrency

5. The different coins available on the market not to have too many to keep track of on top of everything else

6. The size of your investment, so you don't end up pouring all your money into something that either A) tanks before you've even had a chance to see if it works or B) rises beyond your reach with the sort of slow, steady rise that gives you plenty of time to see it coming

7. The development team's roadmap for the future

8. The price of the Cryptocurrency and how much it might be expected to rise or fall over time

9. The value of the Cryptocurrency compared with other cryptocurrencies in circulation
10. The volatility that the currency is likely to have to maximize gains or minimize losses while trading

Once you know what you're going for, you can begin looking at some cryptocurrencies for investment – though this post isn't about picking tokens out of thin air. This way, we won't spend too much time talking about choosing a token that has no essential use case or will go away after you buy it. We'll also be looking at some promising blockchain projects that are already in development, so it won't just be about which crypto tokens are worth buying at the moment. In a nutshell, here are the factors to look at:

1. What geographic markets are the token being targeted?
2. Is there a team behind the project? Is the team experienced, and is it staying power?
3. Does it have an existing product or product-level solution that can help solve a current problem for consumers?
4. Does it involve new technology that could disrupt industries such as supply chains and data management?
5. Is there a community of users behind the project?

6. What is the number of different coins available on the market?
7. How much is your initial investment, and how much can you spend on the initial investment?
8. Which marketplace does the cryptocurrency work on, and why does it need to be implemented here in particular?
9. How is the price of the currency expected to change over time?
10. Are there any significant competitors affecting the price of the currency?

The Criterion to Choose a Cryptocurrency that will Appreciate in Value

The criterion to choose a cryptocurrency that you will appreciate is relatively subjective - but if someone is unsure what to invest in, an introduction might be the best place to start. Additionally, a detailed list of some of the world's most well-known cryptocurrencies is included with some basic information on each coin - helping investors to narrow down their options for investment.

This extensive resource can also serve as a starting point for those looking for a comparative guide. However, it's worth noting that this article does not offer investment advice - instead of providing information on how to get started with cryptocurrencies and enjoy benefits from them once you do. The following is the criteria used to choose a cryptocurrency that will appreciate:

1. Cryptocurrency is open source.

The reason for this is that there's no point in investing in a cryptocurrency that lacks transparency. Open source cryptocurrency ensures the platform it runs on is public knowledge. Therefore you can be thoroughly certain every single aspect of the platform has been looked over by a wide variety of professionals - reducing your risk as an investor. So if you're looking to invest in cryptocurrencies, make sure the currency has open-source code! This eliminates any risk.

2. It has a public blockchain

A public blockchain is a big deal - it ensures transparency, which means that anyone can view every transaction. This sort of 'open ledger' means investors can check up on the current standing of the project they're considering investing in. This means they can see how many coins have been issued, how many are stuck in certain wallets and look over the project's roadmap and development history. A cryptocurrency without a public blockchain is sometimes referred to as a 'centralized' cryptocurrency.

3. It has a fixed supply.

Supply obfuscation is a method of reducing the value of Cryptocurrency by tying its value directly to a certain amount of coins in existence. This is often done by inflating or deflating the coin - making it seem as though there's an ever-increasing supply, when in fact, there isn't. An example of this would be proof-of-stake (PoS), which relies on new coins minted exclusively to reward those who join the network and are therefore effectively granted an initial stake in that currency. Unfortunately, these projects are often mis-sold, with the coins coming with a fixed supply notably touted as a benefit.

4. It has a growing market cap.

A growing market capitalization shows the value of an investment from day one - which means it is a much better starting point than if you were to buy before it was introduced to the investment world. A growing market cap also means that if the currency is "hard-forked," a term that describes when a cryptocurrency is split into two, your holdings will be shared between both resulting currencies - usually at a 1:1 ratio.

5. It has low transaction fees

It makes sense to invest in blockchain technology that enables low transaction fees. There's no point in spending money on an investment that can't be used to its full potential while the currency you're invested in isn't allowing for fast transfers. Investing in cryptocurrencies with fast and affordable transactions ensures you can send funds easily when trading, buying or selling.

6. It's a community project

Cryptocurrencies that are community-centered have a higher chance of surviving - because they rely on the people who invested in them to survive. This means it's more likely that Cryptocurrency with a strong community feel will succeed over competitors who lack a strong following and that the currency will be developed according to its original roadmap.

7. It allows for private transactions

While most open-source cryptocurrencies allow users to remain anonymous, some don't allow for entirely private transactions - making it impossible to move funds without third parties being aware. Therefore, a cryptocurrency that allows for completely private transactions has the highest chance of success.

8. It has reasonable terms for miners

The mining process is an essential part of Cryptocurrency. If it isn't supported in some capacity, it won't make it very far in the world of cryptocurrencies. Unfortunately, some cryptocurrencies have such high fees that they become unviable - primarily because investor funds don't necessarily match up with miners, meaning miners aren't rewarded accordingly. This means investors are left without rewards, and there's little incentive to maintain the currency or develop it further.

9. It has a low energy consumption

Once again, the mining process is essential in ensuring a cryptocurrency's network remains secure and running smoothly. If there's no incentive to mine, miners won't be there to protect the network. This makes it vulnerable to hackers or even groups of miners who can manipulate the chain by creating their coins and then inserting them into the blockchain at a different address - effectively stealing funds from investors.

10. It's easy to use

The more people who are using a cryptocurrency, the more likely it is that development will continue and that trading between users will become available on an international scale. If a cryptocurrency is difficult to use, it can't become widely used. Cryptocurrencies need to be as easy to use as fiat currency to be adopted by the mainstream.

11. It has native support from third parties

The more partnerships a coin has, the higher its value is likely to go - because it means other businesses will begin accepting Cryptocurrency on their platforms. On the other hand, suppose no third-party partners work with a coin. In that case, there will be no incentive for developers to continue developing the platform, and chances are investors won't want anything to do with it either due to safety concerns.

Chapter 11

The Differences Between Bitcoin and Ethereum

1. Bitcoin is electronically traded through the blockchain. A decentralized platform that operates on a public ledger-Bitcoin is not controlled by any central authority and uses peer-to-peer transactions.

2. Ethereum is a blockchain-based platform that enables developers to build and run distributed applications with privacy features and smart contracts.

3. Bitcoin spits out Bitcoins in blocks of twenty-one million as it halts to find the next valid block after ten minutes of mining. Each block is discovered by miners who compete against each other for security while preserving blockchain integrity. However, Ethereum only emits coins after a day's worth of work is completed or two weeks if no new blocks are added to the chain.

4. Bitcoin, a cryptocurrency, was developed by an anonymous programmer, while Ethereum, a blockchain platform, was designed by a 19-year-old Russian-Canadian programmer Vitalik Buterin.

5. Bitcoin is limited to the number of coins created, while Ethereum has a continually increasing supply of coins mined on its platform.

6. The two cryptocurrencies have different blockchain protocols-Bitcoin uses the Proof of work system, which requires miners to find and validate blocks that increase transaction speed. Still, it is energy demanding and expensive to maintain. In contrast, Ethereum uses the Proof of stake protocol which eliminates the need for miners in transactions due to its consensus algorithm called Casper that rewards validators who deposit their Ether coins as stake for validating transactions within blocks.

7. Bitcoin is used primarily as a currency, while Ethereum is used to build more complex smart contracts.

8. Bitcoin has a more significant market cap than both the stock market and gold, with Ethereum having the second-largest market cap of all cryptocurrencies. If it were a country, that would give it the third-highest GDP following China, the United States.

9. The long-term success of Bitcoin or Ethereum hinges on adoption-Bitcoin's primary use case is as a currency, while Ethereum is designed to be utilized with smart contracts. However, Bitcoin has started being adopted

by various international merchants due to its faster processing speed, greater liquidity, and lower transaction fees.

10. The technology to develop cryptocurrencies such as Bitcoin has existed since 1985. Still, the spike in interest in it can be attributed to the rise of digital currencies such as Bitcoin, seen as a hedge against traditional fiat currencies.

11. The major entities focusing on Bitcoin-based cryptocurrencies include the CME Group, CBOE, NASDAQ, and Goldman Sachs. At the same time, Ethereum has only been more aggressively targeted by big Wall St banks since its inception in 2014.

12. Using blockchain technology to develop online platforms for conducting transactions within minutes rather than days or weeks is one area where Bitcoin and Ethereum are being used today, including digital payments such as BitPay, Coinbase, and GoCoin. In contrast, other industries that use blockchains include banking, financial services, and healthcare.

Why Can Ethereum Grow Faster Than Bitcoin?

1. Security – Ethereum uses a PoS where Ethereum holders vote on the next block producer. Meaning it is less centralized than Bitcoin's PoW.

2. Transaction fees – In contrast to Bitcoin, users pay gas (ethereum) to miners for each transaction they wish to have processed and secured by the blockchain.

3. Adoption of ETH as a payment method – With more than one hundred operations made for the trading of ethers on some exchanges, people are coming up with different ways in which they can use their Ethers for payment purposes and not just as an investment vehicle

4. Ethereum's growth – The team and development of Ethereum don't stop as with Bitcoin; the sky's the limit for it.

5. Ethereum's token – Ethereum has a token called Ether, whereas Bitcoin has bitcoin.

6. Not used to pay taxes - While most countries require that you pay taxes on your business profits or investments, there is no absolute requirement to pay taxes on a cryptocurrency earned by mining or trading with coins.

7. Hashrate – With Ethereum's ability to have millions of dollars worth of transactions daily, more miners want to get in and make money out of the "free" transaction fees provided by the ETHCoin/Ethereum network.

8. Proof of stake – Bitcoin is scheduled to change its Proof of work protocol to the POS system, and it can

take a while before they see that transition through to success

9. Ethereum can be used as a store of value for large transactions - We have seen bitcoin that it takes a few days to be transferred or exchanged between wallets. In the case of Ethereum, it's only minutes, if not seconds, before you have your money in an exchange wallet ready for purchasing any other cryptocurrency or token within the exchanges.

10. Ethereum is not strongly controlled by any central authority. This makes it the perfect currency for business owners who want to work with Blockchain technology but don't want to spend too much time on the administration of running a node.

11. Smart Contracts – If you have invested in Bitcoin, Ethereum, or any other cryptocurrency, smart contracts are a nice feature to have. This is due to they can automate processes within your cryptocurrency exchange and make them more transparent. A smart contract is an automated program with conditions and triggers that will run when specific needs are met, such as NASDAQ's system, allowing companies to trade their shares without human interaction.

12. Ethereum's development – With the blockchain being a decentralized and public ledger, every change to the blockchain releases new updates to ensure that all users are kept up to date and don't have any inner

information about what is going on behind the scenes.

13. Privacy of transaction - With its private nature (in contrast with Bitcoin, which is public), Ethereum gives users a lot of privacy when transferring their cryptocurrency between wallets.

14. Blockchain Integration – A way to make currency transactions more efficient and make them easier for businesses and companies.

15. More uses – Ethereum is used for more things than just paying for transaction fees on the blockchain.

16. New projects and coins – Many developers choose to develop their ERC20 tokens, which makes Ethereum even more profitable, albeit in the short term as it has become a saturated market now.

17. Ether's energy consumption is low compared to Bitcoin - And this can be an advantage if you like to keep your mining costs down without losing profits and forging new coins for yourself or your company.

Why Will Bitcoin Always Remain the Most Prominent Cryptocurrency?

Bitcoin remains the most prominent cryptocurrency because it is the most established and popular cryptocurrency.

1. Ethereum has close to the same market cap as Bitcoin, which is only about $20 billion less than Bitcoin's current market cap. It also has a growing user base and recently passed one million transactions in a day for the first time on its blockchain network. Bitcoin, however, continues to dominate with an almost 2 billion dollar lead on Ethereum's market cap and three times the transactions performed than Ethereum.

2. Ripple is also a very popular cryptocurrency. It is only 1/3 the of Bitcoin in terms of market cap, but this is still significant. While Bitcoin remains the most established and widely used cryptocurrency, one thing to note about Ripple is that it has recently made inroads into financial services. If this was to catch on, it could potentially expand the use cases and cause demand for its currency to go up.

3. Speaking of financial services and cryptocurrencies that are more traditional for banks and users who prefer an alternative to mined digital currency, Ripple has already noticed some big names in finance, including Santander Bank, UBS, American Express, etc.

4. Problems in Cryptocurrency Industry

5. Average Joe still doesn't know about cryptocurrency. Bitcoin is popular as the first cryptocurrency, but there are not enough resources to teach people about crypto. This is kind of good for the industry, though. The more obscure and unknown it is, the less likely it

is co-opted by governments or other entities who wish to use it against us.

6. There is a lack of education and accessibility of cryptocurrencies, even for developers and competitors in the technology space. Due to this, many developers are creating similar and competing products at the same time. Only one survives and becomes the best cryptocurrency product available on the market, which will gain mainstream adoption.

7. BTC is not fit to be the future digital cash. BTC transactions can only be confirmed every 10 minutes while the average person wants to make instant payments and send money worldwide in seconds. Other cryptocurrencies have faster transaction times, including Ethereum, Litecoin, Dash, etc. With more adoption of cryptocurrency for daily transactions, there will be a necessity for a currency that has higher transaction speeds like Bitcoin Cash which is 14x faster than Bitcoin currently in terms of confirmation time

8. People want cheap and fast coin through PoW consensus algorithms used by Bitcoin and other leading coins today, so they can use them as payment processors or as an alternative to fiat currencies such as Bitcoin Cash which has deficient fees and high-speed confirmation times

9. The ATM industry is still small, with a few machines in Hong Kong and Japan. If cryptocurrency grows massively, we will see many more ATMs worldwide

being put in place to make it easier to obtain cryptocurrencies such as Bitcoin Cash.

10. Bitcoin has been jumped on by different actors in the market that wish to abuse its popularity and popularity of other cryptos, especially in less popular regions such as China which has recently banned Initial Coin Offerings (ICOs). This move will likely cause China's dominance of the cryptocurrency market cap to decrease significantly.

However, there are still many problems that Bitcoin does not address. There is a demand for faster transactions, lower fees, and most importantly, people want to use cryptocurrency for daily transactions. This will make cryptocurrencies more popular instead of just using them as an investment or a way to send money around the world.

There will likely be more cryptocurrencies in the future to compete with others while offering something new and unique. The use of original cryptocurrency is more of a way to send money than an investment, as bitcoins are not worth much. There is no real monetary value associated with them, making it hard to use as an easy form of payment.

Chapter 12

What Is The Future Of Cryptocurrencies?

The future of cryptocurrencies is difficult to predict. Just as bitcoin's price has risen and fallen dramatically over the last few years, so too have the prices of other cryptocurrencies. For example, bitcoin prices soared in December 2017, then collapsed under pressure from government regulators and a lack of adoption from mainstream markets in 2018. As a result, today, it's hard to say what the future holds for any given cryptocurrency. Still, one thing is inevitable: cryptocurrencies will only continue to grow in popularity thanks to their low costs, lack of third-party interference, ability to facilitate international exchanges without costly fees, and ease of use.

One thing that makes cryptocurrencies so popular is that it's hard to predict their future value. And this is a good thing: cryptocurrencies enable people to control their own money at all times, with no one to answer or block transactions. As a result, Bitcoin is often referred to as "digital gold." Both bitcoin and gold are limited in quantity. But while gold has an annual mining output of about the same volume every year, new bitcoin will cease to be "mined" once we hit the 21 million cap. Besides their fixed quantity, bitcoins and gold have another similarity: they're both highly valued for their ability to hold monetary value.

As a result, the price of these cryptocurrencies will continue to fluctuate. As they do, their demand will rise (when prices are high) and fall (when prices are low). That's no different from other non-monetary assets such as real estate, stocks, or bonds.

Cryptocurrencies are also gaining momentum in countries around the world. Governments and central banks around the globe have taken notice of cryptocurrencies and their potential for undermining traditional methods of payment and transfer. For example, China recently banned financial institutions from engaging in cryptocurrency-related business, while Russia has announced plans to create a national cryptocurrency. Other countries, like South Korea, have promised to implement regulations by 2018.

While the future is still unclear, there are some things that investors and consumers can do to prepare for the cryptocurrency revolution. This includes:

1. Investing in a Digital Wallet.
2. Getting Familiar With Crypto-Markets.

3. Trying Out Some of the Major Cryptocurrencies.

Purchasing cryptocurrencies is more complicated than opening a regular bank account but not by much. First, users need to create a "wallet" like a virtual bank account to send and receive their cryptocurrencies. Then, they also need to connect it with their real-world bank accounts for initial purchases and withdrawals (theoretically, this isn't necessary if you're only using your bitcoin for online purchases).

There are many different wallets available, and they can be installed on mobile devices, computers, or external hard drives. Once the user has a bitcoin wallet, he or she can go online and purchase some bitcoin. (Note: investors should only purchase bitcoin if they know exactly what they are doing; there is something called "pump-and-dump" scams where investors buy coins for the sole purpose of selling them off at higher prices.) Once you've purchased your stash, make sure you have access to a digital wallet to store your cryptocurrency.

You're probably curious about how to make money with cryptocurrencies. In general, digital currencies are still in their early stages of development, so there isn't a lot of action. But that will change as cryptocurrency exchanges continue to open and more companies begin accepting them in place of traditional money. The best way to make money is to invest in the leading cryptocurrencies: bitcoin, ethereum, and litecoin. But remember that the future of cryptocurrencies remains uncertain.

There are other ways to make money, such as mining for new coins or trading on digital currency exchanges. Mining involves investing in powerful computers to solve bitcoin algorithms and recoup a small percentage of their investment (although mining is so challenging, it's no longer possible for individual investors). Trading requires an investor to know how the market works (and know what he or she is doing).

Each cryptocurrency has its wallet address. This includes:

1. Your public address (this is the address that you will share with other users).
2. Your private key (this is your wallet login information).

Whenever any of your users send cryptocurrency, they will appear as a payment in your "Crypto-Portfolio.". When you want to transfer currency to one of your bank accounts, you will need to have that currency listed under "holdings." Next, click on the dropdown menu and select which cryptocurrency you want to transfer. A new window will open up to enter the amount and select which bank account you wish to share.

A variety of other tools are available just for the cryptocurrency world. You can find secure bitcoin wallets, currency charts, exchanges, and other tools that could lead to a more prominent understanding of cryptocurrencies. It's also important to remember that any government or central bank does not regulate these currencies, so their values are solely based on supply and demand.

It's true: Bitcoin is a digital currency created in 2009 (although it didn't receive widespread attention until 2013). It is the largest cryptocurrency, trading hands globally at $7.3 billion at the end of December 2016 (it reached a high of $1,200 in December 2015). Bitcoin uses peer-to-peer technology to operate with no central authority: the payments are made directly between users, without a third party (such as a bank or payment service) getting involved.

Since there is no government backing, Bitcoin could face risks such as fraud and censorship. However, Bitcoins are accepted by thousands of merchants globally, including Overstock.com and TigerDirect.

Contrary to the earlier popular belief, Bitcoin is still not gaining mass adoption according to the latest market trends for several reasons. This note will explain what makes Bitcoin unique from the traditional currency? The key difference between Bitcoin and middle-man-based business models is that Bitcoin operates on decentralized principles. This means the authority for the dynamics of Bitcoin is spread across a network of "miners" and not concentrated in one place. Furthermore, since Bitcoin is peer-to-peer, transactions can only be made on a trust basis between registered and verified individuals.

For example, most financial institutions today rely on middle man banks and other third parties for the transaction to complete successfully. For example, a bank account can only be opened if you have filled out all required documents or if you have proven your identity through several means such as government identification, driver's license, passport, etc.

The Future of Decentralized Applications

Remember, Cryptocurrencies are digital or virtual currencies that use cryptography for security purposes and provide anonymity when dealing with transactions such as transferring money between individuals without revealing their personal information to other parties in the transaction (i.e., vendors). The easiest way to see this is to think of money as a physical object (i.e., a bill, coin, etc.).

Traditional currencies are backed by a government (i.e., the United States dollars or the Euros). Digital currencies aren't backed by anything but rather by mathematical principles that determine quality. These currencies are entirely decentralized, so they aren't regulated by a central bank, and there's no single point of failure for their security. The lack of regulation around these currencies also means that they can surprise governments and traditional banks. Rather than being restricted to one specific purpose (i.e., taking a ride on a public transportation system), cryptocurrencies can be used to pay for goods and services.

The first cryptocurrency was introduced in 2009, and the first one to reach mass adoption was bitcoin. Bitcoin is what's known as an "open source" currency. Bitcoin took off so quickly because of the program that keeps the blockchain (i.e., how blocks are created, linked, and have their contents validated) running: software developers (i.e., you). The developers developed this program to improve their communication ability without using traditional electronic communication methods (i.e., email, SMS text messaging, etc.). In addition, they wanted to test the technology in a real-world setting, so they created it as a cryptocurrency.

Bitcoin was initially a proof-of-concept project that caught the attention of many individuals who saw the potential of moving away from traditional currency and the ability to use it for more than just digital transactions. It caught the attention of shady internet users who could now buy drugs and other illegal services online without having to worry about getting caught.

In 2013, the United States federal government shut down Silk Road (an exchange-traded in illegal drugs) and arrested its founder. The creator went by his online persona, Dread Pirate Roberts. This event helped raise awareness of cryptocurrencies and criminal activity, which is still an issue today.

The future of decentralized applications Now that we understand what a cryptocurrency is, how it works and the people who are developing them, let's talk about why they're essential. The blockchain (which is behind cryptocurrencies) was created by Satoshi Nakamoto (who never revealed his identity) to store and verify data without authorization from a central authority. This means that the blockchain has become an area of interest for companies looking to build software applications that require decentralized applications. These companies are looking for applications where there isn't a single point of failure where hackers can gain access and change or manipulate the data.

Decentralized applications aren't often used by consumers right now, but they're moving toward being mainstream in the coming years. For example, imagine a Wikipedia that can't be changed by the people who maintain it. Imagine not having to trust third parties (i.e., banks) with your money and relying on a decentralized currency. One of the biggest challenges for these currencies moving forward is scalability; the blockchain isn't large enough to support them.

We've also seen cases where companies have raised massive amounts of money through initial coin offerings (or ICOs). For example, Tezos raised more than $200 million in two weeks earlier this year, and EOS expanded a staggering amount of $185 million in just five days this summer. Still, there's no guarantee that these companies will deliver everything they promise in such short periods.

Chapter 13

Cryptocurrency Scams

Scams in Cryptocurrency Trading

Many scams are found in the cryptocurrency marketplace, and each one has a different way of being executed. One technique is by trading bot software on social media websites such as Twitter or Facebook, making market movements using automated scripts. The scammer will give the bots instructions, either pre-programmed or customized to their liking, to trade into various markets to make profits for themselves. The following are documented scams that are commonly seen in the cryptocurrency trading markets.

1. Pre-mined currencies: These cryptocurrencies were created by developers from the start, with a certain number of coins set to be released later. This means that the developers' wallets are filled with pre-mined coins,

and they release these onto the market as they please when it is worth their time or when someone has given them a certain amount of money for this "service." These services often have nothing to do with the development or support of the cryptocurrency. The only thing they are after is your money, and they will try to scam you out of it. They often sell the pre-mined coins for a low price, and then they release more onto the market as an airdrop to "share the wealth." This is another reason why it is crucial to research a cryptocurrency before investing in it. Otherwise, you will find yourself being scammed.

2. Pump & Dump: This scam is just as undesirable as it sounds, and they have been around for years now. They advertise a particular cryptocurrency and make everyone believe that there will be huge returns if you invest in it, or even better if you hold onto your coins until the increasing value of it amongst other investors causes its value to rise. The scammer will then release a large amount of pre-mined coins, which he holds onto for himself while pumping the coin's value to its maximum, or just a few cents. When this happens, he will release more pre-mined coins into the market, and this is often called an "airdrop." There are no markets for these coins - they are released over time by an individual developer or group of developers who hold onto them for their gain. No quality projects should be advertised this way, as there is no way to know how the coin will develop.

3. ICO Scams: Investing in a cryptocurrency is not something you should do on a whim, as you will then

find yourself scammed. An ICO is when a company or an individual releases their cryptocurrency and tries to raise money from investors to develop and launch the coin into the market. This can be seen as a risky venture; after all, if they fail, then they will burn all of their investor's money. It is a relatively new concept, and some of these ICOs have been hit with scams before they are launched. The best way to approach these types of ICO is to research the team behind it, the whitepaper, the concept, and everything else that you can find out. It is highly recommended that you examine an ICO before handing over any money to them!

4. Blockchain Fork: This is a scam that has been used by scammers for many years now in cryptocurrency trading. A blockchain fork occurs when two or more people or companies use the same blockchain, and it splits off into two separate chains. This could be because of mutual agreements between developers or disagreements between developers, which causes the chain to split and form two different blockchains with one coin on each chain. When this happens, the value of the two coins is determined by the markets and will often bear no resemblance to each other. There is a high level of risk involved in this type of scam, and it is highly advised that you avoid it.

5. Ponzi Schemes: Suppose you are not familiar with this particular scam. In that case, you need to be aware that they can be particularly dangerous in cryptocurrency trading, as they tend to be extremely hard to spot because there is no official authority investigating them.

A Ponzi scheme is where individuals or groups of individuals will release their currency and raise money from investors who purchase their coins with another cryptocurrency such as Bitcoin or Ethereum. Then, the individual or group will use the money they have received from investors to trade into other cryptocurrencies such as Ethereum or Bitcoin and profit on their investments. They then take all of the investment money and use it for their gains by trading it into other cryptocurrencies, and when investors start realizing this, they will pull out of the currency in which they invested and cause a panic sell. This means that people will withdraw their funds from the currency they invested in after realizing that there is no way to get their investment back. This causes the value of coins to fall rapidly, causing losses in cryptocurrency trading.

6. Pump & Dump Scams: The final type of scam you need to be aware of in cryptocurrency trading is the pump and dump scam. This is just like the previous scam, but with a few differences. In this situation, a developer will gain popularity amongst investors because he has released a great product or made huge profits from his trading. He then releases many coins he holds onto and makes sure that it rises in value. When this happens, he will sell a portion of his pre-mined coins to raise the price for everyone else and then release more onto the market for trading purposes as an "airdrop."

7. Fake Technology: The last scam that you need to be aware of is related to the technology that is used by cryptocurrency trading. It is effortless for scammers to

get hold of blockchain technology, whitepapers, and other information related to cryptocurrency trading and then use it as part of a scam. A lot of technology has been created to make it so simple for anyone to create their cryptocurrency. Still, some people have managed to find ways around this and are simply making up new cryptocurrencies out of thin air with no real-life backing. This is more common in the early stages of cryptocurrency trading. Certain people will try to release a new cryptocurrency that does not offer any real value and simply gain attention for their project. This is done by making it seem like they are giving away cash, Ethereum, or Bitcoin, but in reality, they are simply getting investors to send them money.

8. No Reputation: Suppose you have been involved in cryptocurrency trading for any amount of time. In that case, you will know that you need to research your coins beforehand and find out the reputation that the developer has with other users on forums. If you do not do this research, then you stand the chance of investing in coins that have a terrible reputation and losing a lot of money. The cryptocurrency market is full of bad press and rumors and good press and rumors, and if you rely on what other people say about a specific coin or developer, you will be putting yourself at risk.

9. Fake Exchanges: The final scam that you need to be aware of is related to cryptocurrency exchanges; fake exchanges are those developers set up to take advantage of investors by stealing their funds. These kinds of exchanges usually present themselves as legitimate

exchanges to trick people into using their service. If you are looking for an exchange, then make sure that you research them first and find out about their reputation from other users on forums and message boards. You should also check with the Better Business Bureau as they have a lot of information about companies or services that have ripped off customers in the past.

10. Sending Funds To The Wrong Address: The final type of scam concerns sending funds to the wrong address. Many cryptocurrencies are not like fiat currencies, where addresses are based on specific characters. Cryptocurrency addresses can be complicated to read or copy, so always try to use a wallet address that you know rather than taking it from someone else. It is also important to note that the address will not be accepted if it is not part of the blockchain, even if someone sends you an address or QR code.

Investing Money Wisely

I hope you have found all of this helpful information, and I would like to encourage everyone to invest in cryptocurrencies continuously. Just because it's a little more complicated than conventional currencies does not mean that you cannot benefit from them; with some research, you can become a successful investor in cryptocurrency. Just remember all of my tips, and don't ever invest anything unless you are 100% sure about what it is and where it will take you.

How to Avoid a Scam in the Cryptocurrency Business

There has been a gradual increase in the number of cryptocurrency scams appearing each day. It can be pretty daunting for those new to this market to tell whether or not an investment opportunity is genuine or a con. This is where this article will help you decipher between legitimate options and fake ones. The following are ways on how to avoid a crypto scam:

1. Do personal research on the project involved.

    This one is very straightforward and can be done in a couple of minutes. You can use search engines to determine whether or not the cryptocurrency you are interested in investing in has an active, used, or abandoned project. This is important because it will help you know whether or not the company running the project has enough people behind it and if they have their project out there in a way that will make them stop creating more problems for themselves or others later on.

2. Consult with everyone around you who has been following this market lately. Another resource you can utilize to avoid scams is that of your peers. You will find many people to talk to, and they will most likely be willing to share their opinion with you since they know more about cryptocurrency than you do. After all, they have been following this market for a more extended period than you have.

3. Do not rush your decision when it comes down to investments that can change your life. Most cryptocurrency scams happen because people are too eager to be the first ones in a project or buy something from an opportunity that might be too good to be true. They want the attractive benefits of cryptocurrencies but do not pay more attention and research on how legitimate these opportunities are. Therefore, you should make sure to avoid rushing into your investment decisions. If it is very urgent for you, try to postpone your decisions and not take action immediately so that you can give ample time to analyze a project or an investment opportunity further.

4. Think before jumping from one project to another. There is a chance that cryptocurrency scams are no longer new to you. This might be why you have become more cautious about what projects are real opportunities and which ones are just an attempt from scammers to take advantage of other people's money. There is a huge possibility that you have already tried an investment opportunity that turned out to be fake. Regardless of that, you have learned many things about the cryptocurrency market, and you are sure to spot a scam immediately when it appears.

5. Avoid telling people that you have money or tokens. The more people know about your investments, the bigger chances you have for scammers to get in touch with you and convince you that they have an investment opportunity that might be too good to be true. Scammers can use your desire to invest in something profitable to

extract more information from you about how much money we own at the moment or what capital we can utilize in investing in other opportunities. This is why you should avoid telling people about how much money you can invest in another project or company, and if you happen to get an opportunity from a person who claims to be part of a cryptocurrency project, do not respond immediately.

It may seem like an obvious thing for your friends or other family members to tell you about possible scams when it comes down to dealing with cryptocurrencies. Still, the truth is that they might not be aware of the potential dangers associated with cryptocurrencies. It would also be beneficial to share your knowledge about scams and how other people get tricked into investing their money in cryptocurrency scams. This is what you can do to help keep cryptocurrency scams away from yourself.

Conclusion

I would like to conclude the book with some of my considerations and thank you for the preference given to me by reading up to this last chapter.

Since cryptocurrencies are practically universally recognized currencies now, they can be used worldwide and with a large type and variety of users, without any problems. One of the reasons why investing in cryptocurrencies can be advantageous nowadays is also constituted by the processing costs: these, for each operation, are significantly reduced, unlike what happens for other types of currency, which imply much higher rates and management costs.

I think it is worth investing in cryptocurrencies. They are a powerful tool going through exponential growth. Following the Covid-19 Pandemic that has affected the entire globe, many states have irreversibly started to print money. Well, maybe they printed too much money, and this could turn into inflation.

But one must ask: what exactly is inflation?

Just to give you an idea, The United States of America has printed more money in one month than in two centuries. Marvelous, isn't it?

"The United States of America printed more money in June 2020 than in two centuries of history. Last month, the U.S. budget deficit of USD 864 billion was larger than the total debt accumulated between 1776 and 1979."

The Fed itself, using all the tools at its disposal to deal with the pandemic, including printing money, has kept interest rates close to zero and is buying USD 120 billion worth of assets per month.

However, analysts believe that inflation is indeed there but that it is "hidden" in asset prices rather than consumer prices, given the role of money issuance in supporting the stock market during the pandemic. Given the analysis I have just done, I think that humanity is undoubtedly at the beginning of a new era, before and after the pandemic. For this reason, I believe that the future is increasingly directed to virtual currencies and that over time they will be increasingly solid and consolidated. Good luck and happy investing!